Dressage Riding

RICHARD L. WÄTJEN

DRESSAGE RIDING

A Guide for the Training of Horse and Rider

Translated from the German by
DR. V. SALOSCHIN

Original Foreword by
COLONEL V. D. S. WILLIAMS, O.B.E.

Foreword to 7th Edition by
OBERBEREITER FRANZ ROCHOWANSKY

Original translation by Dr V. Saloschin
Revised and edited by Daphne Machin Goodall
after the German 7th edition which was revised and
expanded by Major-General Albert Stecken,
President of the Committee for Dressage in the
German Olympic Committee for Equitation.

J. A. ALLEN & CO.
1 LOWER GROSVENOR PLACE
LONDON, S.W.1

First published 1958

by J. A. Allen & Co Ltd.

1 Lower Grosvenor Place

London SW1W 0EL

Second Edition 1961

Reprinted 1965

Reprinted 1966

Reprinted 1969

Reprinted 1973

First published in this edition (Revised) 1979

Wätjen, Richard Lacey
Dressage riding – 3rd revised ed.
1. Dressage
I. Title
636.1'08'86   SF309.5   77-30491

ISBN 0-85131-275-6

Translated from Fifth Revised Edition

© Paul Parey, Hamburg and Berlin

Printed in Great Britain by
Lewis Reprints Ltd.
Member of Brown Knight & Truscott Group
London and Tonbridge

Foreword

Many books on riding have been published in this country in recent years.

These books may be divided into two categories. The first, which includes the majority, whose authors are more in their element seated at their desks than in the saddle, whose knowledge is based on reading the works of others and on theories that are not substantiated by practice.

The second category, of which there are alas too few, whose authors have spent a lifetime in the saddle and have put on paper the result of their own experiences; whose theories are not only based on the works of the past masters but on a life of practical horsemanship.

This book belongs to the second category and as such should find a place on the book shelf of every student of equitation.

R. L. Wätjen received his early training at the Spanish Riding School in Vienna and has since that time produced many horses of Grand Prix Standard.

He has proved himself not only as a trainer of Classical horses but also as a first class instructor. He was employed as instructor to the British Team which competed at the Olympic Games at Helsinki in 1952 and there is no doubt that the seeds that he sowed during that time contributed to the success of our team when they won the Gold Medal in the Three Day Event at the Olympic Games in Stockholm in 1956.

This book, originally written in German, has been translated by Dr. V. Saloschin, who not only speaks the German and English languages fluently but is himself a highly experienced horseman.

He is to be congratulated on performing most excellently the difficult task of translating the German text into English which is a pleasure to read and easy to understand without changing in any way the meaning of the original text.

I wish the author every success and I hope the book will be read and studied by everyone interested in the correct training of the RIDING HORSE.

V. D. S. WILLIAMS

Foreword to the 7th Edition

For several decades and even before the Second World War I knew Richard Watjen as a very distinguished dressage rider and dressage instructor.

Richard Watjen spent many of his formative years at the Spanish Riding School of Vienna, first as a pupil and later as an amateur guest instructor. It was during these visits to the 'school' that Oberbereiter Polak and Richard Watjen became very close friends, a friendship which lasted until their death.

Herr Oberbereiter Polak – who was also my teacher at the Spanish Riding School of Vienna – always spoke very highly of Richard Watjen's many skills and excellent understanding of the dressage art.

In this book the Author has shown how clear and concise are the riding aids. His description and definitions are a model of correctness and simplicity. In many other books on dressage and horsemanship, similar instructions are usually made so complicated that they more often than not confuse rather than help the rider.

I highly recommend this excellent book on dressage riding and training and consider it a great honour to be invited to write the foreword to this new edition of an established work on the art of horsemanship and dressage. May I also wish all riders much pleasure and success in their studies and applications of dressage in its many different stages.

Franz Rochowansky
Oberbereiter i.P.
Spanische Reitschule WIEN

Contents

PART ONE

Elementary Dressage
('Campagne' School)

Contents

PART TWO
Haute École

Illustrations

BIBLIOGRAPHY

Abé, R. A.: In memoriam Richard L. Wätjen. In: Georg, 1966, Heft 3, S. 2 u. 3.

Braun-Marsani: Berühmte Reiter erzählen. II. Band. Limpert-Verlag 1941, S. 104–137.

Menzendorf, W.: Reitsport. Ein Bildband 1900–1972. Textliche Bearbeitung von H-J. von Killisch-Horn. 1972, Verlag Paul Parey, Berlin und Hamburg.

Seunig, W.: Meister der Reitkunst und ihre Wege. 1960, Erich Hoffmann Verlag, Heidenheim.

Wätjen, R. L.: Erinnerungen an die Weiner Hofreitschule. In: St. Georg Almanach 1953, S. 68–71.

Introduction

The fact that the fourth edition of my book on Dressage, 'The Art of Riding in Word and Picture', was sold out in six months, makes a fifth edition necessary. I have chosen as a title for this new edition, 'Dressage Riding'. The last edition was completely revised, with special reference to the training of teams for four Olympic Games—Amsterdam 1928, Berlin 1936, London 1948, and Helsinki 1952—this edition contains supplementary material.

It is my intention, by keeping this text book short and simple, to give a brief, reliable and clear survey of dressage so that it may be easily understood by every rider without laborious study.

In this book I have drawn on my own experience of over forty years in the theory and practice of schooling horses and instructing pupils, in order to help those who are professionally connected with the training of horses and riders.

By themselves, theoretical principles and hints can never lead to success; to bear fruit they must be allied, in practice, to the skill and feeling of the rider. I have designed my book accordingly, and I shall be very pleased if it contributes to the proper training of horse and rider, thereby increasing the general knowledge of the art of riding.

The training of the riding horse must be adapted to the individual ability of the horse by systematic and progressive training. It makes no difference whether the horse will later be used for hacking, show jumping, or as a school horse. Elementary schooling ('campagne' school) which develops the natural abilities of the horse, must come first and then lead on to the higher form of dressage. Only a rider or trainer who has learned by long, intensive study, both in theory and practice, the methodical progressive training of the horse, will be able to reach this goal. In this sense my book should be a guide.

From my earliest youth onwards I was in the fortunate position of being able to devote myself to all types of riding. This, my ruling passion, stemmed from my innate love of horses. After I had studied the principles of riding, I devoted my whole life to this art. Neither set-backs nor successes prevented me from working and learning, in order to reach, physically and mentally, that ability which is expected from a true horseman and trainer.

Through the generosity of my parents I was able to acquire the necessary theoretical knowledge by working at well-known Government studs, at Trakehnen in East Prussia and at Graditz, which was the former German National Stud. They also helped me to realize my great ambition to join the Spanish Riding School in Vienna.

From 1910 to 1916 I had the privilege of being accepted in this High School of Riding as a pupil. From 1916 to 1921 I was honoured in being allowed to train and ride the wonderful Lipizzaner stallions as a guest and amateur instructor.

Because I had the good fortune to work at this famous institution, I was able to learn from the great masters, who were the pillars of this unique school. There, I also had an opportunity of observing the best riders from many countries who were seconded to Vienna, to exchange views with them, to learn from them, and to study their methods of riding.

In 1925 I made up my mind to build up in Berlin a scheme for professionally training horses and riders. My work was rewarded for many years by the numerous successes achieved by my pupils and myself at all the big shows in Germany and also in international events abroad.

Everything I have learned during the long years of my riding experience, I have tried to put down in this book for the *profit of other riders. Numerous horses of various breeds, in many different movements of both Elementary Dressage and High School are used to illustrate the book. In these photographs I am riding horses which I myself trained.*

PART ONE

Elementary Dressage
('Campagne' School)

GENERAL PRINCIPLES

EFORE discussing in detail the methodical training of a dressage horse, I intend to make a few remarks in answer to that question which is so often asked: *Why school and train a horse in dressage?*

The reply can be given in one single sentence. *To increase the capability and appearance of the horse and to prolong its ability to work.*

We have learned from history and literature that the art of riding was already highly valued in the days of Xenophon. After a rapid decline, caused by wars and other upheavals, the proper schooling of the horse blossomed again, especially in Italy and France, in the sixteenth century. One can learn from the literature of the period that the training of the school horse, even up to the movements of *Haute École*, served to increase the efficiency of the war horse.

The famous riding masters in the reign of Louis XIII considerably influenced the development of the art of riding in France.

In England, Germany and Austria, Riding Academies were founded at the Courts of kings and princes, where, for instance, masters such as the Duke of Newcastle, who died in 1675, and the German, Loehneysen, who lived around 1600, devoted themselves to the art of riding in theory and practice.

During the next century this art developed more and more. The famous book by Guerinière, who died in 1751, is evidence of this. With the foundation of the 'Spanish Riding Stables' and the creation of the Royal Stud at Lipizza, a new training ground for the art of riding was created. In 1735 a wonderful baroque building was erected in the Viennese Hofburg, the most beautiful riding school in the world, which even today remains the only place where the true classical art of riding is taught and practised. The architect was the famous Fischer von Erlach. After the school horses and equipment were saved through the initiative of the American, General Patton, the school found a temporary home at Wels on the Danube. It did not return until 1955 to Vienna, its traditional home.

The Viennese Riding School practises not only the art of dressage in its highest form for its own sake, but as a means of testing the quality of the stallions at Lipizza.* Thus the merits of these stallions as school horses have greatly influenced their selection for stud. Only those whose conformation, temperament and proper gait had been thoroughly tested, found a place in the famous Lipizza stud. From this we learn that, dating from olden times, the proper training of the school horse has increased both its efficiency and its beauty. But one must always remember that this can only be true if the training is based on methodical work which concentrates on gymnastic development, and which achieves the highest proficiency in completely natural abilities, without being forced or stooping to the use of tricks. Then the horses will suffer no harm; on the contrary, they will be able to fulfil their work and tasks for many more years than they would have done without proper training. They will gain suppleness by the correct development of the muscles. The best proof of this is to be seen in the stallions of the Spanish Riding School, which are able to execute on and above the ground, the most difficult movements of the school, without any strain to their legs, even at a very advanced age. This is

*After 1918 the former Austrian stud Lipizza was incorporated in Italy and later, after the second World War, in Yugoslavia. The stallions are now bred at Piber in Western Styria.

only possible if, in their youth, the stallions are not trained by brute force or asked to do too much, but are gradually brought to perfection in the course of a sound dressage training based on the right principles.

Great masters of the German art of riding were, amongst others, Seeger and Steinbrecht ('The Gymnasium of the Horse'). In the opinion of the latter, the aim of dressage is the development and regulation of the natural powers of the horse; he also takes into consideration the mental abilities and their improvement through systematic training. The same system applies today. Steinbrecht also says that one should point out to every rider: 'Ride your horse forward and keep it straight.'

A further proof of how dressage training increases stamina could be seen in the cavalry horses of the German and Austrian armies. They retained their stamina up to a very advanced age.

The increasing interest in dressage and various combined training events gives us, in these days, the chance to test the capabilities of our horses, thus providing an invaluable aid in choosing the proper material for breeding purposes.

Every rider, breeder and horse lover should endeavour to understand the principles of the art of riding; without this understanding they cannot expect to bring their horses up to a higher standard of training.

MENTAL AND PHYSICAL CHARACTERISTICS OF THE RIDER

The most important conditions for the dressage rider who wants to obtain high position in the art of riding, are a genuine love of horses, an honest and sincere enthusiasm and a will of iron to enable him to achieve the highest results.

The ideal is to train the horse and so obtain harmony and perfection in all movements between rider and horse so that they appear to be as one. Horse and rider should master all movements without compulsion or force and be able to execute without effort the most difficult exercise of the classical Haute École. This is the goal and the result of long hours of work demanding the highest standard of an individual.

It is the honest love of working with a horse that should give the dressage rider the constant aim of trying to obtain perfection and not the ambition of obtaining great successes and a lot of prizes at shows. A rider who is simply interested in winning prizes is like a 'pot-hunter' who wants to be successful by any means without heart or feeling for his horse.

This kind of rider will never feel that the art of riding can be one of the greatest of experiences and will never claim to be called a master. Only the love of the work can help the rider through the years with their many disappointments and give him the strength, not to give up but to keep on trying. The laurels of horsemanship can be achieved only by years of work and experience combined with enormous patience which prevents explosions of temperament and the use of force.

Of course, even during his early years the individual has to feel the ambition and passion to begin serious work. A proper education of the young rider can begin only at around twelve years of age, after the youngster has enjoyed learning the basics of horsemanship during his everyday contact with horses.

During the first 3–5 years of his education he must learn to have an absolutely correct and flexible seat that is not dependent upon the horse's movements and he must be so physically trained that there is no stiffness and a correct use of the aids can be given at any time.

It is only when the rider is as one with his horse, has got the necessary sensitivity and possesses a horseman's tact that attention must be paid to his mental education. The rider must be absolutely certain if he/she wants to devote his/her life to the art of riding.

The work of instructor and dressage rider is for those who take it seriously, both educational and character-building. Only those who are absolutely determined and refuse to be deterred and stick to their principles can hope for success in the long run. Only an experienced self-possessed individual who is capable of relinquishing outward success or even ostensible success, can achieve the maturity that is necessary to become a "master".

THE RIDER'S SEAT

It is an old saying that 'a rider can be judged by his seat'. The result of a good seat will always be a good influence upon the horse. It is every rider's duty to improve his seat and to make it firmer by taking every opportunity of observing better riders, and correcting himself.

The rider should hold himself upright and in a natural position, with his back braced, and sitting well down in the middle of the saddle at its lowest point, which is in fact the centre of gravity. The rider's knees must be drawn back so far that the inside of the thigh lies flat against the saddle. He should hold his feet naturally in the stirrups with the heels well down and his feet almost parallel to the ground. The lower part of the legs should hang down loosely, the inside part in light contact with the horse's body, so that the leg aid can be applied quietly and calmly, the leg gently touching the side of the horse. In the dressage seat, which is being discussed here, the stirrup leather should be so long that it is possible for the rider when stretching his legs, to make gentle contact with the horse's body with his calves. Stirrups that are too long cause restless legs, and this leads to an unsteady seat. Stirrups that are too short prevent the rider from sitting gracefully down in the saddle and he appears to be sitting on a chair. To a certain extent the length of the stirrup depends on the horse's conformation and its progress in training.

The upper arm should almost form a right angle to the forearm. The rider should hold his hands about four inches away from his body, so that when the wrists are slightly turned inwards, the little fingers should be opposite each other; the hands vertical, and fairly close together. The rider should hold his shoulders square, letting them drop naturally. The upper arms should rest gently against the rider's body, so that they form a support for his hands, enabling them to exercise a calm and continual influence. The rider's back should be straight, but not rigid and stiff, so that the simultaneous leg and rein aids are transferred through the rider's back directly to the back of his mount. The combination of a straight back and supple hip joints enables the rider to adapt himself to the horse's movements. He should sit quietly but firmly, independent of the movements of his horse. Hands, with pliable wrists, must remain as calm and steady as possible. Otherwise the pace and the following of movement will suffer, with the mouth becoming insensitive and not, as so many think, active. The same applies to the legs. Constant tapping is useless, even detrimental, since the steadiness of the seat suffers. The horse also grows accustomed to this continuous tapping and becomes indifferent to normal aids. Furthermore every aid should be applied with the upper part of the body held steady.

Exaggerated weight aids should be avoided, as this disturbs the communication between the back of the rider and the back of the horse, thus upsetting at the outset, a proper influence on the horse. Proper weight aids, or balance, are obtained by an increased bracing of the back, or by moving the shoulders slightly forward or backward and shifting the weight very slightly to the right and left; in other words, following the movements of the horse. The bracing of the back and the seat of the rider act on the horse's back muscles.

In all turns, special attention should be paid to the shoulders of the rider always remaining parallel to the shoulders of the horse. A dropping of the inside hip should be strictly avoided. Spurs should only be applied very rarely to reinforce the leg aids. Constant use of spurs leads to a faulty seat.

The horse should form himself under the influence of the rider's seat. The much discussed supple seat should not be confused with sloppiness. Each rider should endeavour to hold himself correctly; that is, he should be supple and never rigid. Even if, in the beginning, his seat appears somewhat rigid, it will become gradually supple, graceful and natural by continual practice and suitable exercises. A faulty seat can never be corrected by suppleness; suppleness is the result only of long practice.

Only an absolutely firm yet completely supple seat can produce a sensitive feeling and lead to the proper independent influence of the various aids.

The rider's seat and position in the saddle should make

a smart impression and at the same time produce an effortless influence on the horse.

The rider should always hold his head erect and look forward above the head of his horse. His chin should never be stretched forward, as this would lead to cramped shoulders, resulting in a bad influence on the driving aids.

THE AIDS

One differentiates between *Leg Aids*, *Rein Aids*, *Whip Aids and Weight Aids*.

The fundamental condition for the correct application of any aids is a firm seat, completely independent of the movement of the horse. The rider must also control his own limbs so that there can be no unintended rein or leg aids.

The *art of riding* and the *harmony between horse and rider* entirely depend on the *correct application of leg and rein aids*; that is, of *driving* and *restraining* which are dependent on each other. The rider should never forget that the driving aids predominate, and that lively horses especially must be ridden with sufficient driving aids. The leg aids should always be applied by the legs of the rider making light, steady contact with the horse's side but without any pressure from the calves. The calmer the legs, the better the horse will respond. Flapping with the legs is unnecessary and ugly; it has a disquieting effect on nervous horses, and makes lazy horses more numb and insensitive. Depending upon its position, the leg can act sideways, restraining or driving forward. When in correct position on the girth, the leg acts in a driving way. To achieve a sideways, driving, or restraining effect the leg has to be applied further back, but hardly more than one hands breadth behind the girth. The degree of the leg aid

8

has either the effect of driving the horse to the side or of restraining it.

Should the horse not react sufficiently to the properly applied leg aids the rider should influence his horse with the spurs. If the spurs are not too frequently applied, but —when necessary—with energy, the horse will sufficiently react to the leg aids. *A rider should never be induced to give spur or leg aids when angered.* A properly considered punishment is more effective and does not make the horse stubborn. A very slight aid with the spur can be applied to increase the energy of the horse to a greater engagement of the hocks, but as punishment the rider should hardly ever make use of the spurs. In order to maintain the sensitiveness and reaction to the rider's leg, the accomplished rider will rarely resort to the use of spurs. One should only use sharp spurs occasionally on a sluggish horse as they are inclined to make a free-going horse restive.

The leg aids are always supported by the *weight aids*. This phrase 'weight aid' can easily lead to misunderstanding. The weight aid is nothing more than a stronger bracing of the back, or following the movement of the horse. The quieter and more supple the rider keeps the upper part of his body, the easier his horse will react to all aids. The correct weight aid consists of putting more weight on one seat bone. To drop the hip is a bad fault.

In considering *rein aids*, one has to differentiate between the *opposing*, the *restraining* and the *giving* action of the reins.

The *opposing aids* consist of no more than a firm contact, and should on no account exert a pulling effect.

The *restraining aids* must influence the horse by an increased bracing of the back and a firmer action on the reins by the rider's wrist and forearm, the upper arm remaining in contact with the body, thus influencing the back muscles of the horse.

The *giving aids* should allow the horse more freedom by a lightening of the hands.

The rein aids must never disturb the constant, steady support and the supple communication between the rider's hand and the horse's mouth. The rider should not try to support the movement by the aid of the reins; this never leads to true success. Leg and back aids must always be predominant. The horse must learn to move in self carriage and must only be *guided* and not pulled by the rider. If the hands are held closely together in the correct position, with supple wrists and a braced back, it will be possible to limit the rein aids to the guidance of the horse and the regulation of the pace. *The rider must never try to turn his horse by passing his hand over from one side to the other. The rider's hand must always act on one side of the horse only, and must never try to support the other hand by crossing over the withers.*

All rein aids can act only from forwards to backwards and upwards or vice versa, but must never act sideways. If the horse seeks too strong a support from the hand, short *arrêts* (a taking and giving of the reins), may be applied as a punishment or an enforcement. These *arrêts* should be used very seldom and may only be applied from a contact, but never from a loose rein, as this would merely result in a jerking of the mouth. After such an *arrêt* the rider's hand should go back into its old position and should endeavour to achieve a supple, steady contact. As mentioned earlier, *arrêts*, like spurs, are used only as a punishment and should therefore be seldom applied. By a clever usage of the leg, back and rein aids the rider should be able to achieve a proper balance of his horse without punishment. For the application of rein aids it is important to have:

1. The hand in the right position, with supple wrists and a correct position of the lower and upper part of the arms.

2. The proper length of the reins, which enables the rider by more or less bracing the back, to act on the horse's back.

The only object of the *whip aid* is to reinforce the leg aid. In time the whip aid should be reduced to a minimum, as well-trained horses should be able to execute all figures and turns without the aid of the whip.

BRIDLING RULES

Bridling rules are very closely connected with horsemanship and are very important. It is therefore correct to say that a thorough knowledge of these rules is an absolute necessity for every rider, for only with their aid can he properly train his mount. Methodical bridling, suited to the peculiarities of the horse, is of the greatest importance for progress in training. Bad bridling can easily spoil a promising young horse at the start of his training.

As I presume the reader is acquainted with the general rules of bridling, I only intend to mention the most important points.

The young horse should be fitted with a head-stall, to which a snaffle bit—not too thin—is attached. It is essential when the head-stall is placed in position that the snaffle is adjusted in such a manner that it touches the corners of the mouth, but without pulling them up. If the bit is adjusted too high it will cut or rub the corners of the mouth when one rides the horse with contact. On the other hand, a snaffle which is fixed too low, will enable the horse to move the bit up and down with its tongue, thereby acquiring bad habits such as putting the tongue out, or over the bit, at the outset. It is advisable to fit a noseband to the snaffle. I would suggest a dropped nose-band, adjusted with the chin straps below the snaffle mouth-piece, thus preventing the horse from opening its mouth. It should not be too tight, however, for the horse must still be able to champ the bit. Discretion must continue to be used in adjusting it throughout the whole of the training.

After the horse is completely balanced, accepts the bit and has learned to execute the ordinary movements in the different paces while ridden in a snaffle, a double bridle can be introduced. A correctly fitted bridle with curb should be fixed so that the bridoon (snaffle bit)—as already mentioned—is neither too high nor too low.

Attention should be paid to the choice of a sufficiently wide curb-bit, with a space of about a quarter inch on each side of the horse's mouth so that the top arms of the curb-bit do not pinch the horse's cheeks when the curb rein is properly used.

The curb-bit should be so fixed that it is about on a level with the curb chain groove. The thickness of the mouth-piece should be suited to the sensitiveness of the horse's mouth. Generally, the use of a thick mouth-piece with not too high a port in the centre piece is recommended. The use of thinner mouth-pieces with higher ports should only be chosen for especially insensitive horses, and those with bad tongue habits.

The curb chain should be fitted so that it lies exactly

in the curb chain groove. When the curb reins are properly used the cheeks should form an angle of about 45 degrees with the horse's mouth.

AUXILIARY REINS

Generally speaking the rider should endeavour to train his horse without auxiliary reins. As the name already implies, these reins should only be used to assist in certain work during the training period of the horse. I only want to mention two kinds of auxiliary reins that are most frequently used—the martingale and the running rein.

The martingale, in my opinion, cannot be considered as a proper aid in the training of a dressage horse. It is only used with nervous and excitable horses in hacking, hunting, cross-country riding and jumping, if they are inclined to toss their heads or resist the bit.

The running reins, however, if correctly applied, can be used as an aid for dressage training. But the rider who proposes to use running reins must have great experience and skill in their use for, if wrongly applied, they can do considerably more harm than good. The object of using the running rein is to ensure that a horse, which tries to avoid the collection by throwing its head up, is forced well *forward* in an even head and neck position with a proper contact. In this way the horse becomes used to accepting the bit in the different movements without becoming unbalanced; the running reins, used in conjunction with the snaffle rein, permit the rider to ride his horse freely forward with a quiet restraining hand.

It is of great importance that the rider should *on no account* try to *force* the horse by means of the running rein into a collection beyond its capacity. It is only advisable to apply the running rein when the young horse has learnt on the snaffle to respond to the driving aids of the rider and to accept the bit. The object of the running rein is, as already mentioned, not to force the horse into a certain position. The actual connection with the horse's mouth must be sought by the rider's hand with the snaffle rein, so that the running rein only serves as a kind of reserve rein, to prevent the horse from accepting the bit by resisting with its head and neck. The rider will only be permanently successful when using the running rein, if he *drives* his horse into the proper head and neck position, at the same time restraining with the snaffle rein only. The running rein should only be used as a reserve rein, but not as a means of attempting a forced collection.

A well-trained dressage horse must always be presented well collected and without running reins; for if the rider cannot keep his horse collected without running reins, it is proof that the horse has not been trained in the proper way.

The running rein is not only of great help with horses who are above the bit, holding heads too high with noses poked out, but also with horses who are tossing their heads and thus, without a running rein, making a collection impossible. Furthermore, the running rein also greatly assists in raising the head and neck, as the rider is in a position to achieve this through the increased driving aids; the horse is not then in a position to make a collection impossible by resisting with its head and neck. As a rule one should only use these running reins whilst *correcting spoilt horses*, or with horses which have acquired bad habits by a too hurried training. With horses which have been trained in a correct, systematic and progressive way, one never needs running reins, and the rider should not use them as they would be damaging rather than advantageous.

The running reins which are buckled together in the middle, like snaffle reins, should each be about eight feet long. It is advisable to have them slightly narrower than the usual snaffle reins, so that the rider can always distinctly feel the degree of contact with the horse's mouth, compared with the snaffle reins. At the end of each running rein, there is a loop which is drawn through the girth above the buckles.

WORK ON THE LUNGE

Before one mounts a young horse, it is trained on the lunge. Since this kind of work has rarely been described in print, and I consider correct lunging to be very important, I should like to deal with it in some detail.

One can, of course, start to train a young horse without previous work on the lunge. But this preparatory work, correctly executed, makes the training on horse-back very much easier and, what is most important, conserves the strength of the young horse.

The object of training is to teach obedience without burdening the horse with the weight of the rider. In this way the young animal finds confidence, it learns to relax in its movements and develops its muscles, regulating and improving its gait at the same time.

This work, correctly carried out, should be executed by one person alone, as lunge and whip aids should act simultaneously like rein and leg aids. However, for young horses it is advisable to have the help of an assistant at the start. The horse should be saddled and bridled with a snaffle. A surcingle should be put over the saddle to which the side reins are attached. It is essential to use a cavesson, as fixing the lunge in the snaffle rings has a bad effect on the horse's mouth. It is advisable to have three rings on each side of the surcingle, so as to be able to fix the side reins in a higher or lower position as may be necessary. Whether the side reins should be fixed to the higher or lower rings, depends on whether the individual horse is inclined to carry its head too high, or whether it is over or behind the bit. Under no circumstances should the side reins be too short or fixed too low, as this would create a short neck, thus hindering the proper use of the hocks and hind legs. The carriage of the head and neck depends on the conformation and on the natural movement of the horse. One cannot lay down a definite rule. The ultimate aim, which can only be gradually achieved, is an unrestrained neck, forming a harmonious curve to the poll, with the head slightly in front of the perpendicular.

A young horse should learn to carry its head in a proper position by adapting this carriage to the various movements. A slight inward bend can gradually be achieved by shortening the inside rein a little.* One has continuously to observe whether the side reins are in a proper position, and the lengthening or shortening has to be done at the right moment. At the walk, the side reins must always be longer and never tight, otherwise the freedom of the walk will suffer. At the trot, and later at the canter, the young horse must learn to relax, and to move quietly forward. Only very gradually, when the horse is accustomed to working on the lunge for longer periods, and has learned the proper balance through strengthening the hindquarters, can one start to shorten the

*Some riding masters, such as Col. Podhajsky, think this unnecessary, and liable to bend the horse at the neck only, instead of through the whole length of its body.

reins and try to achieve the first stage of collection. The horse should then be carrying its head higher, with the neck rising from the withers, bent at the poll with the highest point always lying between the ears.

The lunge should be held in the hand on which the trainer intends to work his horse. This work must obviously be practised equally on both reins. The horse's attention should be called to the whip which the trainer holds with an out-stretched arm pointing towards the horse's flank. Horses which tend to move outwards should be taught to accept the lunge by taking and giving; horses which tend to move inwards must be kept back on the proper circle by slight aids of the whip given from behind and moving downwards to the shoulder. The lash must, of course, be long enough to reach the horse. The voice is of great importance; quiet, but distinct commands without raising the voice are what is needed. Great patience must always be shown, especially with excitable horses. Special attention should be paid to the regularity of the horse's paces; for this, half halts (see page 26) are used. Sudden and rough aids must be avoided.

Progress will only be achieved by working at the same pace, without a sudden increase or decrease of the pace, and by maintaining a steady head and neck carriage.

For this stage of training, lunge and whip aids are given simultaneously, as are the rein and leg aids, which come later, so that the horse is just as obedient on the lunge as under the rider.

The trainer, turning around on his own axis, remains on one spot in the centre of the circle, keeping the elbow of the arm holding the lunge close to his body, in the same position as when riding, with the upper arm almost at a right angle to the lower arm. Strict attention should be paid to keeping an even contact with the horse's mouth, corresponding to the feel of the reins when riding. Lunge and whip should be used to induce the horse to move around the same circle with long regular strides. The trainer should always be in a line with the horse's head, and should not stand in front of the horse. The aids given with the lunge should not be too frequent as this tends to make a horse indifferent and numb, as in riding.

The trainer must always reward a young horse with praise, making the most of it and giving it tit-bits.

Sometimes slight *arrêts* (shaking the lunge up and down) are effective if applied with discretion.

For older horses which have learnt bad habits, as for example, that of carrying the head too low, a bearing rein should be fitted to *correct* this position. The bearing rein is attached left and right on to the snaffle ring and then taken up through rings on a level with the brow band, then to the girth. The bearing-rein will be fastened to a ring at the middle of the girth near the pommel of the saddle and there it can be shortened or lengthened by means of a buckle. It is most important that the horse's head is not brought up too high as otherwise the oscillation of the back and push from the hindquarters will suffer. The aforesaid horizontal line from the horse's nose must not be raised higher than the hip bones.

Generally speaking the use of a bearing-rein should be avoided. It should be used only as an aid to correct horses that have been spoilt.

Naturally the horse must be worked equally on both reins and when the horse has learnt to be obedient and has acquired the necessary suppleness on both reins, the stage has been reached when it can learn to accept the rider.

The rider should be very gently lifted by the assistant into the saddle, while the young horse is held by the trainer. At the beginning the horse has to learn to carry the weight of the rider, who must sit very passively without any rein or leg aids. Very gradually, the rider starts to influence the young horse with legs and reins and, if necessary, with light taps of the whip.

Whereas the lunge trainer always acts in a passive way, the rider gradually tries to achieve a contact with the reins by means of the driving aids, and gets his horse used to the legs and whip aids. At the end of the first lessons one should be able to dispense with the lunge and proceed in riding without it.

TRAINING YOUNG HORSES

The horse that has been taught on the lunge to respond to rein and leg aids can now be ridden without side reins. The three most important points are: *To ride forward; to put the horse straight* on a long rein; and during the preliminary stages, *to see the horse is not 'collected'*.

From the beginning it is essential that the horse learns to react willingly to the driving aids, and to recover its natural balance under the weight of the rider, without at this stage, considering its head and neck position. Very gradually the rider can seek for a contact at the trot. Rising is advisable. He has to be extremely careful to put the horse very gently to the bit with increased driving aids. The quietly restraining hands put the horse straight and try to find equal contact with both reins. In this way the young horse learns by a gentle pressure from both legs, helped by the whip, to stretch itself to the bit.

When the horse is gaining strength and becoming more supple in the back, one can start to ride with a slight collection, but only at the trot. At the walk, one has to ride the young horse on a long rein without contact, until it has learnt to accept the bit at the trot and at the canter, on a straight line and in simple turns. One should not start work at the canter (which loosens up some horses more quickly) until the horse is obedient at the trot, and responds to the rider's aids. Striking off to the canter should be executed from the trot, preferably on a big circle or in the corner of a *manège*, with the aid of the legs, supported by the whip on the inside shoulder. If the horse starts to rush away at the trot, one should bring it back to the ordinary trot with half halts, and then repeat the aids for the striking off. From the beginning, the rider should drive his horse well forward with impulsion at a fairly strong canter.

The rider should also make certain that the horse learns to move '*straight*' on one track and at this early stage of training the rider should not try to obtain a shortened stride. Gradually, the horse will learn, depending on its conformation and natural suppleness, to respond willingly to the aids of the rider at the trot and canter, and to accept the bit without resistance.

At the end of each lesson one has to practise a fairly long period of walk on the long rein and also frequent halts with very little contact. Dismounting, mounting, and standing quietly should also be practised frequently.

How long the rider has to work the young horse in this way depends entirely upon the age and strength of the horse. Under no circumstances should the rider ask too much before the horse has made a good start in developing its natural paces.

THE ORDINARY COLLECTION of the RIDING HORSE ('CAMPAGNE' SCHOOL)

The collection and proper head carriage of a well-trained riding horse cannot be mechanically determined, but must always be adapted to the conformation and individuality of each horse.

The horse's neck has to be raised so that its nose is approximately on a horizontal line with the hips, the nose and forehead slightly deviating from the vertical. The highest point of the neck rising from the withers, should lie between the ears. The horse must carry itself by its own impulsion, without seeking support from the rider's hand. Shortening the neck should be strictly avoided as it deprives the horse of its natural impulsion and free forward movement.

This position enables the saddle horse to execute all the movements and turns required by the rider, by means of his aids and by maintaining a steady light contact with the horse's mouth.

As already mentioned, the horse's carriage should be the result of proper forward movement and impulsion. A forced collection is highly detrimental, as it prevents the horse from engaging its hocks and using the hindquarters in the correct manner.

To collect a horse means creating suppleness and lightness, thereby producing a relaxation of the horse's back muscles. This is achieved by the driving aids of legs and seat, and by the restraining hands. The raising of head and neck is the natural consequence. A proof of a true collection is a free, unrestrained and energetic forward movement.

Proper head carriage, gradually developed from this forward movement, will lead to the correct development of the horse's muscles. The horse can then move freely forward without any difficulty in self carriage.

In obtaining collection the greatest part is played by the rider's seat; his braced back must form an unchangeable, supple, and yet firm connection with the horse's back. His hands must be steady and supple, offering the required resistance so that the animating aids are checked by the bit, and thus represent a limited resistance, by which the horse—relaxing in neck and back—is collected. If, as a result of the simultaneous application of the driving aids and of the restraining rein aids, the horse becomes relaxed, the hands must be slightly drawn back, while remaining light and supple, so that the reins are in gentle communication with the horse's mouth. By means of the driving aids the horse is collected from the rear to the front. This collection must be supplemented and maintained again and again by riding straight on and freely forward. In each pace, walk, trot or canter, the urge to ride forward must predominate, and the horse, relaxed in its movements, must endeavour to champ the bit in slight communication with the pliable hands. This carriage of the horse is the foundation of all further training. A horse that has systematically learned to adopt this carriage under his rider, and who is able to advance in it without restraint, will improve in every respect and can then be trained for all other purposes.

There is no doubt of the bad consequences which follow a forced, unnatural collection gained by artificial means (mainly running reins) which one so often observes. As a result of this excessive pressure of the bit on the jaw, the horse is more or less forced to bend its neck and to adopt a head position which is in no way in harmony with the engagement of the hind-quarters. The consequence of continuing to ride in this manner is, obviously, a bad head carriage. The horse bends at the neck and is *not* bent at the poll, thus making a relaxation of the back muscles and the proper influence of the hind-quarters—the forward drive from behind, through the horse, to the bit—impossible. As soon as these artificial aids are abandoned, it will be apparent that the desired progress has not been achieved. The development of the muscles, created by systematic work, is missing. The horse, free from pain, will now offer more resistance than before. One is obliged sooner or later again to apply force and it will never be possible by this method to achieve an ideal collection which can be permanently maintained without any effort.

How different if the horse has learned by his own impulsion and by systematic progressive training to relax in his back.

The proper head carriage is the result of a free forward movement. The horse has not been forced by tricks and artificial means into an unnatural position.

A horse trained in this manner can be ridden even by a weaker rider and this is the best possible proof of systematic work.

Of course, the horse's conformation and suitability play a major part. A horse with a good conformation will adopt the proper head carriage with almost no effort and will execute with ease and willingness whatever is asked of it.

In the case of a difficult horse, where the rider must compensate for the physical deficiencies by training, the value of the method described above will be particularly appreciated, for in this case it is impossible to maintain an ideal head carriage by sheer strength and through the application of artificial means.

When collecting at a halt one must at first be satisfied with a slight raising of the neck, for it is of great importance that the horse is taught not to resist, but to relax its neck, by the rider holding his hands in a lower position and using animating aids. Side stepping and stepping back must be prevented by the rider's back and leg aids, which have to exercise a quiet and steadying influence. A higher degree of collection at a halt can only be asked of horses that have already learned to be collected and supple in free forward movements created by their own impulsion. This is only possible with a horse in an advanced stage of training. At the beginning, collection at the halt should be required only for short periods.

HALF AND FULL HALTS

First, we must distinguish between the half and the full halts.

The *half halt* is executed in the transition from a more extended to a shorter movement. The most important factor in all halts is to carry them out—in the truest sense of the word—from the *rear to the front*. A halt should never be performed without simultaneous *driving aids*. The hindquarters must always be fixed and engaged by the back and seat of the rider. The horse must catch the forward impulsion with its hindquarters. The raising of head and neck entirely depends on the respective pace and on the stage of the horse's training. Correctly executed half halts strengthen the hindquarters and make them supple. The more advanced the horse is in the stage of training the more important is the execution of correct halts.

Correct application and execution form an essential part of the successful training. The half halts enable a fluent transition from one movement and one pace to another, thus achieving the required suppleness of the horse.

The half halt is obtained by the rein aid, which must be varied in strength and duration with the capability of the horse. On a well trained horse the firmer closing of the fingers, in connection with an increased contact for a fraction of a second should suffice to renew and increase collection. The half halts, in conjunction with simultaneous driving aids, regulate and maintain the horse's balance. Corresponding to its suppleness and lightness these half halts must be applied more or less frequently in order to create and maintain the collection and to regulate the pace. It is obvious that they can only be applied if the horse is on the bit. Rough and jerky rein aids are to be condemned as unworthy of a good horseman. Unfortunately they are often seen on the exercise ground and even at big shows. Such actions have nothing to do with the true art of riding and are only applied by riders who are forcing their horses to execute certain movements which are contrary to the gymnastic training and suppleness of the horse.

The *full halt* brings the horse to a standstill. It must be brought about by several previous half halts according to the previous pace. The halt must always be executed on one track.

From a proper halt one is able to proceed into a new movement with a smooth transition, providing the horse is supple, relaxed in the back, and well on the bit. After the halt has been established the rider must be careful to avoid a shortening of the horse's neck, but must be light with his hands and give slightly with the reins in order to prevent the horse from stretching out his hind legs.

The transition to the full halt as with the half halt, is achieved by the rider using driving aids in pushing the hindlegs forward and also in the halt by keeping his legs

25

in light contact with the horse's body. The rider's upper body must not be behind the perpendicular in conjunction with the horse's back.

DEFINITION OF THE VARIOUS PACES

In order to train a horse efficiently a thorough knowledge of the movements and different paces is essential.

COLLECTED WALK. The horse is well collected, it places its hindlegs well under its body, the neck is supple and sufficiently raised from the withers, and bent at the poll. Its walk should be absolutely even, with steps which are not too long, but accentuated. It must, at any time, be ready to proceed into an extended pace.

ORDINARY WALK. In this the horse is less collected. It should advance with an even, light contact on the bit. The hindlegs should step slightly over the tracks of the forelegs gaining ground in forward direction. It should be an absolutely even walk with regular pronounced steps.

EXTENDED WALK. The horse should walk well forward with lively, even steps, the hindlegs should overstep the tracks of the forelegs by at least the breadth of a hoof. The horse should stretch its neck well forward in an unrestrained position, still being lightly on the bit, and walking well forward without hurrying. The rider should pay great attention to seeing that the hindlegs follow straight and evenly, lightness and self carriage being most important.

FREE WALK ON A LOOSE REIN. The horse should gain still more ground; its head and neck must be well stretched forward. There should be no contact through the rein, which remains absolutely loose, yet the horse must not deviate to the right or left.

ORDINARY WORKING TROT. The rider should choose the pace at which his mount can be easily kept in balance in a cadenced trot in order to achieve a proper sequence of the steps; he keeps a light contact with the reins. The head and neck carriage and the pace should depend on the stage of training the horse has reached.

COLLECTED TROT. The horse should move with high steps, not gaining much ground, in perfect collection, and with a pronounced cadence. The action of the hind-legs must be as energetically executed as in the extended paces, but the impulsion is now directed more upwards than forwards. The horse has to produce lively, rhythmical steps; a drawn out passage-like step is considered a bad fault.

STRONG TROT. The horse should not be quite as collected as before, but proceed with long, elastic and even strides, gaining ground in a forward direction, the hocks well engaged and maintaining good self carriage and suppleness. An exaggerated stretching of the forelegs is wrong, and is a sign of tension.

EXTENDED TROT. The impulsion should be still stronger. The horse should extend in a bigger frame, with the hindlegs engaged to the utmost. Self carriage and suppleness are the proof as to whether this movement is properly executed.

ORDINARY CANTER. The rider has to choose the pace at which he can best maintain his horse's balance. The head and neck carriage is the same as at the ordinary trot.

COLLECTED CANTER. This should be developed from the ordinary canter. By the increased engagement of the hocks and the increased raising of the head and neck the horse becomes more compressed, so that each stride is executed with full strength and highest impulsion, the horse not gaining much ground. Here also, as at the collected trot, the impulsion goes upwards. True collection is necessary.

EXTENDED CANTER. Here the strides should be longer and unrestricted without, however, being hasty. The rider asks for less collection.

GALLOP. This can only be properly executed out of doors. The horse should achieve the highest development of its cantering abilities in an absolutely natural position, without pulling.

The execution, from the extended canter and extended trot in the dressage arena, as required in the Grand Prix, can only be performed by a horse that is completely balanced and fully trained.

WALK, TROT, CANTER

In order to collect a horse at a walk it must walk absolutely straight forward and then be collected as described above. When the horse has learned to flex and has acquired a proper head position with vertical forehead and nose, and is light in the mouth, then the rider should drive it forward with both legs on a straight line. With braced back, and elbows at his sides, the rider should restrain with the reins, so that this restraint is transferred from the rider's wrists, elbows and lower part of the back, to the back of the horse. It must be strictly observed that the hand *restrains*, in the precise sense of the word, and does not pull back, so that the driving aid is greater than the restraining one. In this way the horse is *guided* into the proper head carriage from the rear to the front, and not *dragged* into it. The time spent in riding at a collected walk remains entirely dependent on the horse's individual reaction. If the horse finds it difficult, the rider should be satisfied with a short period, repeating the exercise a little later, until the horse has learned to maintain the desired position. If the horse is supple in walking, then one starts to develop the trot from the walk in the manner described above. The rider must be particularly careful to see that the sequence of the paces is correct, and that collection is not achieved by upsetting the true, steady walk.

The correctly ridden walk is an excellent way of working the horse. It should be noted, however, that in no other movement does faulty response to the reins and the horse's unfitness show as clearly in uneven strides, as in the walk. Above all, too much collection spoils the natural length of the stride.

When developing the extended walk, the horse must be so completely between the rider's leg and hand, that pressure from the legs and yielding of the hands, that immediately and without a single faulty pace it extends the stride. At the same time the neck is stretched without losing contact.

The collected walk should never be practised too soon and only then when suppleness is assured. Otherwise there is real danger that the walk drags and is not true. In addition, it should be asked for, for only a short period.

During working pauses the free walk on a free rein should be ridden. Horses should not toss their heads or hurry with uneven steps. The free walk shows if the early work had been correctly done.

When the horse has learnt to submit at the ordinary walk, one can commence as shown, the exercise from the walk to the trot.

Where young horses are concerned, it is particularly important to keep them on a *straight line* and to *proceed on one track*. Side stepping, and wrong flexion of the neck must be avoided from the outset by appropriate leg and rein aids. Always keep your horse straight, endeavour to maintain an even contact and ride with impulsion—straight forward. Furthermore, sharp turns should be avoided at the beginning; one should not ride too much into the corners, as the young horse finds them difficult to take while maintaining a proper head and neck position. The greatest importance should be attached to *the correct sequence and regularity of the paces; this is the foundation of all precise movements of a well-trained riding horse.*

One should never try to achieve collection by forcing the head and neck into a certain position, by pressing the hands downwards or by pulling back with the reins. A proper head and neck position is the result of the driving aids towards the restraining hands. If a horse is inclined to over-bend or to lean in this position on the bit, the rider has to drive his horse well forward, increasing the pace, and maintaining a proper sequence by firmer action of back and leg, and with very light hands. One will then succeed in raising its head and lengthening the neck.

When the young horse has reached the stage that it goes forward perfectly relaxed at an ordinary trot, exercises at the strong trot and collected trot may be commenced.

At the strong trot the horse goes forward with long, light energetic strides whereby carriage and balance are most apparent.

The exercises at the strong trot are practised with short repetitions developing from the ordinary trot. Especially through the changes, i.e. on the long side of the school or on the diagonals, when increased leg pressure brings the hindquarters under the horse so that it learns to *lengthen the strides* and must produce light springy action from the forelegs so that the forefeet fall where they are pointing. An exaggerated stretching of the foreleg whereby usually insufficient ground is covered at the trot, is quite false although often to be seen. The hind legs must implicitly follow diagonally without deviating. The horse must learn, with oscillating back and supple neck, to let itself swing forwards when given sharp effective driving aids whilst being restrained gently with the reins.

The strong trot is the best test of a correct and proper training and its execution together with the transitions essential for a correct evaluation of the standard of dressage. At the beginning the horse must not be driven on too much otherwise the result will be irregular action from the hindlegs and a leaning on the bit. One must be patient and very gradually demand the full development from the ordinary trot. A horse that is forced forward and restrained will certainly produce a long stride but this is full of tension and makes an impression only on the layman.

In the same way exercises in the collected trot should be performed properly and one should never ask too much. At the collected trot, the horse is much more collected and should produce an elevated short trot combined with great cadence. The hindlegs must follow energetically with a springy action, whereby, however, the impulsion is directed upwards instead of forwards.

Energetic paces, rhythm and suppleness are the characteristics of the collected trot. Uneven passage-type steps are proof of tensions and incorrect schooling. The hindlegs are made to work correctly by the rhythmical collection of the ordinary trot, this exercise is repeated frequently, and by riding on circles, by exact bends in the corners, and the tempo shortened so that the collected trot is gradually developed.

In developing the collected trot, it is an advantage to practice the movement for short periods as a transition from the strong trot. The necessary heightened push or activity from the legs is thus made use of. By means of the half halt using leg pressure at the same time, the horse is pushed together and learns, with active paces to carry itself in a higher form of collection. Here too, as with the strong trot it takes a long time before the horse has learnt to go in a beautiful collected trot.

If the horse is well on the bit at the walk and trot the rider can start with the work at the canter. The rider can teach the horse to strike or lead off in various ways, either on a fairly large circle with increased driving aids until the horse strikes off, or in taking a corner in the *manège,* when one can easily strike off with the aids of the legs combined with tapping the whip on the inside shoulder. The inside leg of the rider should act on the girth, the outside leg slightly behind it; the position is maintained by the outside rein. When striking off a young horse into a canter, the animal should be well on the bit before applying the driving aids. Half halts with the outside rein prevent the horse from rushing on and pressing to the inside, without influencing the proper head and neck position. At the same moment the leg aids must be given correctly and with sufficient strength. In most cases the horse will then strike off into the desired canter. When it is on the proper leg, the rider has to support and maintain the canter with both legs but mainly with the *inside* one. An exaggerated seat, weight aids and support with the rein should be avoided, as these would restrain the impulsion and impair the sensitiveness of a young horse.

The rider should not hurry in any way when teaching his horse to canter, for the more obedient it is at the walk and trot, and the more it has learned to relax under its rider, the easier will it accept the aids for striking off and maintaining the canter.

The pace must be suited to the individual abilities of the horse; it should move freely forward so that it can readily keep going. If it strikes off on the wrong leg it must be gradually brought back to a trot, and the exercise repeated. When a horse has willingly learned to strike off from the trot into a canter, it can be practised from the walk, but it must be well on the bit beforehand. Here, also, the rider should be satisfied with a few exercises and a short period. In the elementary stages little attention should be paid to the head and neck position. Only when it strikes off *easily* and *without any effort* should the rider gradually endeavour to obtain a proper head and neck carriage. In all paces the horse should move freely *forward* and with *impulsion*, as only then will it use its hind-quarters in a proper way, thus acquiring a *good head carriage* and *collection*.

Even in the elementary stages the rider must train his horse to canter straight forward, *on one track*. It must always have enough freedom to move freely and naturally forward. The rider's inside leg must remain firmly on the girth and continually *support the horse's inside hindleg*.

The result of correctly applied driving and restraining aids is that the horse's hocks are well engaged, and in this way the rider gradually achieves the desired collection. If a too early collection is attempted, with an insufficient engagement of the hindquarters, the result will be that the horse does not canter on one track. In striking off it is particularly important to see that the horse moves well *forward* and does not hesitatingly canter on two tracks.

The increase to the strong canter and extended canter must be gentle and smooth. The driving aids must not be sudden. The horse should be light on the bit and with the increase in stride should remain with its head in the correct position. The freer the tempo the more the rider goes with it from the seat. Even so he has to be careful that the horse when developing the full capacity of its gallop, and in spite of a definite acceptance of the bit, it can be brought submissively to a halt through the half halt.

The transition to the collected canter is achieved by the rider gradually catching the canter stride without checking the horse suddenly. If the collected canter is commenced too early or exclusively achieved by increased aids from the reins, then faulty uneven or hurried canter movements can easily occur or even a false footfall (four-time). The halts and submission must be kept in time with the canter strides. The hands may be more passive when the horse has acquired a reliable self-carriage whilst in complete submission. The legs should stimulate the hind legs to a regular and active stride so that the collected canter is executed in an assured, energetic and elevated style.

For the young horse it is easier to carry the weight of the rider when he is 'rising at the trot'. The rider should go on doing it until his horse has reached the first stage of balance and when the back muscles are developed.

For hacking and riding across country one usually rises at the trot, as it is far less tiring for horse and rider than sitting.

For the rising trot the rider does not remain seated at each stride; he rises from the saddle at each alternate stride. He should keep his knees flat on the saddle without pressing and put his weight on the stirrups with ankles and heels well down. Under no circumstances should he permit the lower part of the leg to go in front of the vertical; in coming down in the saddle he must keep his legs slightly behind it.

The rider should carry the upper part of the body somewhat forward, thus following the movement of the horse.

Trotting on the off or near hindleg, or on the left or right diagonal, are the distinguishing characteristics of this pace.

In the school or outside arena, the rider should *be out of the saddle* when his horse swings the inside shoulder forward and come down in the saddle when the horse puts the inside hindleg and outside foreleg to the ground. While on the right rein, the rider sits in the saddle when the off hindleg and near foreleg, called the left diagonal, come to the ground, and on the left rein when the near hindleg and off foreleg, called the right diagonal, come to the ground. The reason for coming down in the saddle on the inside hindleg is to achieve an increased and energetic engagement of the inside hock by the driving aids of the rider, especially in cornering and circling. When changing rein the rider must change the diagonal without interrupting the cadence.

The rider should not rise too high from the saddle. It looks ugly and the rider loses contact with the back of the horse, thus creating stiffness. For transition from walk to trot or trot to canter and back again, the rider should sit for at least two or three strides. To change the diagonal, the rider should sit for one stride, then rise again.

There are exceptional occasions when one uses the other diagonal for a special reason; for instance, on the left rein one can use the left diagonal in order to influence the off hindleg more, but one should never continue using the same diagonal on both reins.

It is most important to train the young horse equally on both diagonals and to change frequently even when hacking, otherwise the horse will become stiff and one-sided, with the result that the horse strikes off easier with one foreleg leading than with the other one.

The rider soon gets the feel for the proper diagonal and the smooth change, but he must be taught the correct method of rising at the trot in order to use the driving and restraining aids in a proper way, thus improving his horse's balance.

While rising at the trot the rider should also maintain a light, even contact with the horse's mouth and he must take great care to ride freely forward. The correct sequence of the paces and proper cadence is most important.

When the young horse has made sufficient progress at the ordinary trot to move freely forward and maintain a natural head carriage, one can start work at the *extended* and *collected* trot.

At the extended trot the horse should move forward, gaining ground with long elastic strides, while being well on the bit. Self carriage and balance are the two important factors.

The extended trot should be developed from the ordinary trot, and should only be practised for short periods. Proper transitions from the ordinary to the extended trot are very important, and the rider should make full use of the long sides and the diagonal of the riding school to teach his horse to lengthen its strides. By engaging the hindlegs with increased driving aids, the rider induces the horse to use his forelegs freely from the shoulders. The artificial cramped stretching of the forelegs, whereby the strides do not gain sufficient ground is wrong and unnatural. The hindlegs must follow the diagonal without stepping sideways or moving too much apart. The increased driving aids, together with the restraining influence of the hands, teach the horse to increase the pace with an elastic back and a supple head and neck position. The extended trot is always the result of methodical training on sound principles. Smooth transitions provide one of the best proofs of a well trained horse.

At the beginning the rider should not use too strong driving aids, as this results in uneven paces of the hindlegs and in the horse leaning on the bit. With these movements the rider should not hurry, but only gradually demand the full development of the extended trot. A horse driven forward by force and held back by the rein might show long strides, but the movement is tense and only the uninitiated gain the impression that the horse is in an advanced stage of training. (Plates III and IV.)

With the *collected trot* the rider should not start too early. The horse should show elevated steps, not gaining much ground, and it should be in good collection, and show proper rhythm with the maximum impulsion; in other words, this is the proper dressage position. The hindlegs should be well engaged, but the impulsion goes upwards, instead of forwards, as in the extended movements; the horse becomes more compressed. Lively steps, proper cadence and suppleness are the criterion of a collected trot. Dragging- and passage-like steps are signs of tension and unsystematic work.

In developing the collected trot it is of great advantage to practise it for a short spell in the transition from the extended trot. The rider then makes use of the impulsion created by the extended trot. With half halts and simultaneous *driving aids* the horse becomes more collected, thus learning to move with higher head carriage and with lively, animated steps. As with the extended trot, it takes some time before the horse can execute a true collected trot.

Not until the horse has learned to move correctly at the extended and collected trot, with proper smooth transitions, can one start to obtain the maximum extension from the extended trot. The position of the rider's hand should be lower, so that the horse can gain more support from it, and by carrying the head and neck slightly lower, is able to achieve the complete development of its trotting ability. This maximum extension should not be practised too often, and should only be regarded as the result of correct training at the extended and collected trot.

At this maximum extension, as well as at the very extended canter, the utmost engagement of the hocks and greatest impulsion are imperative and so is a proper lengthening of the neck. Under no condition should a firmer contact and a shortening of the neck be apparent. The rider should be able to drive his horse forward with light contact, but with increased impulsion, gaining maximum ground in self carriage.

THE REIN BACK

A well-trained riding horse should rein back calmly and willingly. The properly collected horse, standing in a correct position, can be reined back without difficulty by the increased, restraining action of both reins. Special care should be taken by the rider's leg aids to see that the horse cannot swing its quarters sideways, but that it steps backwards *in a straight line*. Where young horses are concerned the rider should be satisfied with a few steps only and he should ensure that these are not hasty, but calmly follow each other, step by step, in two-time by pairs of diagonals. Simultaneous rein aids acting on the hindlegs should be applied. When the horse is reining back care must be taken not to shorten the neck; that can easily happen by too firm a contact with the reins. Otherwise the horse gets into the habit of creeping back with an arched back. It is not advisable to repeat these exercises too frequently. Special care should be taken to see that the horse *stands quietly* after reining back. These movements when correctly executed, increase the suppleness of the hindquarters and the lightness of the head carriage. If a horse shows great difficulty in reining back, it is advisable to teach him at first from the ground.

Where young horses are concerned, the rider, using a light contact and corresponding driving aids, should first make the horse walk half a step forward. He should then make his horse rein back with the aid of the reins and re-straining leg aids. In this way one avoids the pulling back that is so often observed. Only after one has reached an advanced degree of suppleness can the rein back be correctly executed from the stand-still.

With young horses which show considerable difficulty in reining back one should practise frequent halts and turns on the forehand.

TURNS, FIGURES

To increase the suppleness of the horse and to teach it to respond to the influence of the rider through his leg and rein aids, one should practise turns, figures and movements on two tracks.

The usual turns and figures required from a riding horse are those *on one track:* changing the rein, down and across the centre, turns to the right and left, riding on a circle,

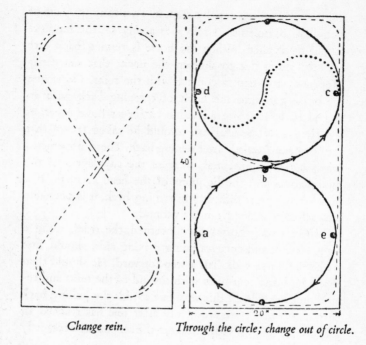

Change rein. *Through the circle; change out of circle.*

out of the circle and changes through the circle, turns on the forehand and on the haunches, small circles, serpentines, figures of eight, half pirouettes, etc.

All these turns and figures, should *at first* be practised at the ordinary walk, as this is the *pace* at which a horse finds it easiest to execute them. It is particularly important that the horse performs these movements at a lively, even walk, gaining ground, with the imprints of the hindlegs overstepping those of the forelegs. In this way, the horse walks exactly on *one* track, and learns to avoid swinging the hindquarters to the right or left. In all turns and figures the horse must be in an absolutely straight position and

40

PLATE I. *The Correct Seat—The Author*

PLATE II. *The Author with Tolerant on The Lunge*   PLATE III. *Ordinary Working Trot*

PLATE IV. *Extended Trot*   PLATE V. *Collected Trot*

PLATE VI.
Reins in one Hand

PLATE VII.
"Tolerant"
5-year-old
Chestnut Gelding,
Ordinary Canter

PLATE VIII. *Extended Canter*

PLATE IX
Left Half Pass

Right Half Pass

PLATE X. *The Author on World-famous Wotan*

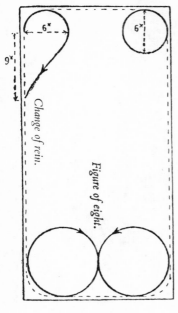

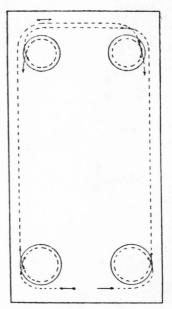

Turns in corner.   *Small circles.*

bent in its length, according to the degree of the turn. The horse is correctly bent if it responds to the inside rein and leg aids, but at the same time finds a support on the outside rein, its neck being well fixed at the withers. In this way it adopts a slight flexion of the whole vertebral column. The degree of the flexion is determined by that of the turn.

The neck, rising from the withers, should *only* be bent to such an extent that the highest point of the neck lies between the ears, so that the rider can just see the inside eyelashes. The inside hindleg, influenced by the rider's inside leg, creates a slight bend in the ribs, helped by the

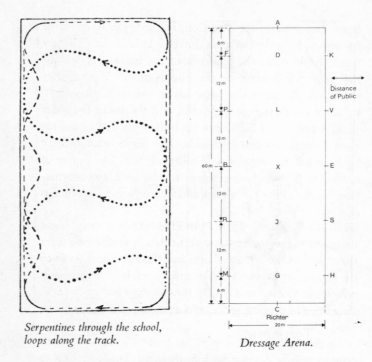

Serpentines through the school, loops along the track.

Dressage Arena.

restraining influence of the outside leg and the steady support with the outside rein. The outside rein is predominant and determines the degree of the turn. An exaggerated bend hinders the correct sequence of the paces. Very often horses have a tendency to shorten their strides in turning; it is therefore important that the rider applies sufficient driving aids with both legs before each turn and thus increases the collection and secures the following of the hindquarters. To avoid the hindquarters deviating from the proper line, the corresponding leg must exercise a stronger influence. It is essential that the rider's hands remain very still. The rein aids should only guide the

42

horse and indicate the direction, but it is the function of the legs to keep the horse on the straight line. An unsteady hand would upset the sequence of the paces and prevent the proper following of the hindquarters. The shorter the turns, the more the horse has to use its hindquarters, in other words engage the hocks, and the more the rider must maintain the balance of his horse by a proper collection through leg and back aids. The horse must execute all turns and figures in a well collected state. The degree of collection is entirely dependent on the horse's conformation, and it is the rider's tact and feeling which determines this collection.

THE TURN ON THE FOREHAND is a very good exercise for the young horse and rider. It teaches the rider the action of the unilateral aids and the horse gets used to the proper application of these influences. It is a movement which the rider continuously uses in the hunting field, in opening and closing gates, and avoiding hounds on the road.

At the halt the rider puts his horse to the bit, maintaining a light contact with both reins. The horse has to stand quietly and squarely on all four legs. Then the rider gives his horse a slight position to the side to which it is turning. The rider's inside leg (in the turn to the right, the right leg) behind the girth drives the hindquarters step by step round the forehand; the inside foreleg (in the turn to the right, the off foreleg) is the pivoting leg. The inside rein (the right rein) indicates the direction, the outside (left) rein acts in a restraining way, maintaining the position and regulating the action of the inside rein. The inside hindleg (here the off one) steps over and in front of the outside hindleg (the near one). The rider's outside leg (the left one) which has a restraining influence, slightly behind the girth, receives the impulsion from the inside (right) leg and regulates the movement step by step in order to avoid the hindlegs rushing round. During and after the turn the rider prevents a creeping back through the use of the driving aids of his own back and legs. Stepping forward is prevented by the outside (left) rein. The same sequence applies to the turn on the forehand to the left.

A proper rhythm and even steps are essential. As soon as the movement is finished the rider should proceed on a straight line.

One should not practise this exercise too often, as it puts the weight of the rider on the forehand, but it is indispensable in the preliminary stage of training. Also, for horses who are showing difficulties in reining back, it is a very useful preparation, as well as for their lateral work.

Only after the young horse has learned to execute the turns at a walk whilst well on the bit, should the rider start to practise these movements at the ordinary trot. It is important that the horse must *first* have learned to trot *straight on, well on the bit*. One should start with the work on a circle and with larger turns, gradually proceeding to smaller circles and turns as the training progresses. It is of *fundamental importance* that in all turns and figures the *proper cadence* and *liveliness* at the trot is maintained. The driving aids must prevent the shortening of the pace and the dragging of the hindquarters. The smaller and narrower the turn, the more must the horse be well collected before the beginning of the turn, and ready to respond willingly to the rider's aids. Before turning from the straight line for a turn or for a circle, the rider must create suppleness and impulsion from the hindquarters, so that he can maintain in the actual turn a lively cadenced trot, a proper collection and the appropriate flexion. The *shoulders of the rider* must always be *parallel to the shoulders of the horse*, the hips parallel to the horse's hips (dropping of the inside hip must be avoided); half halts and driving aids have to be applied alternatively.

For all turns and figures the correct *guidance* is of particular importance. The rein aids should be executed in the direction of the rider's body, and, as already mentioned, they should act with the elbows in slight contact with the body, and by the braced back on the horse's back muscles. The horse should be in the full sense of the word *turned and not thrown around,* so that it moves in a position properly adapted to the turn, bent in the ribs, which can be achieved by a correct guidance with the reins. In the actual turn the horse must be more bent with the inside rein, the outside rein supporting and regulating the position, the flexion and the turn. The outside rein is always *predominant,* supported by the inside driving and the outside restraining leg. The horse more or less receives the direction from the inside rein, according to the diameter of the turn. The restraining (outside) rein should act in the direction towards the rider's body, thereby enabling the horse to bend in the turn; should the outside rein be applied sideways, then the horse would be thrown round. The communicating action of leg and rein aids is most important. The horse should always be influenced by the driving aids according to the degree of collection. The centre of gravity (which varies in the different paces) should always be in the middle of the horse. If the centre of gravity is lost, the rider should *not try* to regain the proper balance *by forced collection,* but by applying the driving aids and increasing the pace, thus creating impulsion and collection. The horse moves *in*

45

proper balance if it *executes all turns and figures with an even, light contact, retaining a steady head and neck position; it must not look for an excessive support in the mouth and must respond easily and willingly to the rider's leg and rein aids.* In all turns the inside leg is predominant, as it acts on the horse's inside hindleg which has to support in the turn the weight of the horse's body, and must therefore be brought well forward.

If the young horse is properly schooled at the walk and at the trot so that it is supple in the different turns and willingly responds to the rider's aids in a proper collection, then it can start work at the canter. One cannot fix a definite pattern when and to what degree this work should be executed in regard to collection, flexion and position, as this mainly depends on the conformation, breed and temperament of the horse. With some horses an intensive work at the canter is very advisable for the relaxation of the limbs and muscles, and the resulting suppleness, especially with well bred or thoroughbred horses.

In the further process of training, the work at the canter must be developed to such a degree that the horse gradually learns to maintain the canter in a proper collection, flexion and position. The smaller the turns the more the canter has to be shortened, and the collection and raising of the head and neck increased. The rider has always to pay attention to ensure that the canter is properly developed with impulsion from the hindquarters, and that the same sequence of the paces is maintained. The more the horse gains strength and its balance is improved, the better it will learn to canter in self carriage, and to execute all turns in proper collection and flexion. In practising these turns, great care should be taken to maintain the natural impulsion which should never be sacrificed for the sake of collection and position. The *execution of correct turns is only the result of a systematic training on sound principles.*

THE TURNS ON THE HAUNCHES are executed at the walk, trot and canter.

At the walk and trot these turns are performed in walking steps, whereas at the canter the horse maintains the correct sequence of the canter in short, very collected strides, in the smallest possible half circle (pirouetting around the inside hindleg).

The well collected horse is led around in proper head and neck position and with slight driving aids; the outside rein is restraining. The rider's inside leg keeps the inside (pivoting) leg in its place, whereas the outside leg prevents the deviating of the hindleg from the track. The inside pivoting hindleg does not remain firmly fixed to the ground, but moves round naturally whilst retaining its original position on the ground. Creeping back is avoided by the rider's well braced back and by supporting leg aids. In the half pirouettes (short about-turns) the horse should not be thrown around. This turn should be performed step by step without loss of balance, around a spot which is near to the position of the inside hindleg.

The pirouettes at the canter belong to the higher school of training and will be dealt with in the second part of this book.

MOVEMENT ON TWO TRACKS

The rider should not start the work on two tracks until his horse is well collected and supple, and able to move on an absolutely straight line at the walk and shortened trot. The object of this movement is to increase the lightness and suppleness of the horse and to obtain a higher degree of obedience. These exercises improve the activity of the hindlegs, and the horse becomes more responsive to the rider's leg and rein aids. The two track movements in question are: *Shoulder-in, Travers and Renvers.*

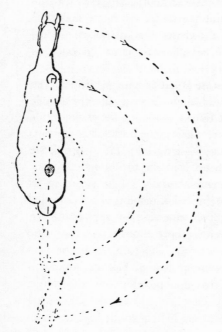

Half Pirouette to the right; turn on the haunches.   *Shoulder-in Right.*

The horse should proceed, slightly flexed, and with his forelegs and hindlegs on *two* tracks. The sidewards position must not be increased or decreased according to the will of the horse, but *the two tracks must remain absolutely parallel to each other.* The sidewards position should not be more than 30 degrees, if one visualises the angle between the horse's back and the outside line of the track, thus the forehand being about one step inside the school (from the position of the outside hindleg to the inside frontleg). An exception is the half pass (across the arena) where the horse should move almost parallel to the track. The *forehand must always lead* and the hindquarters must be kept well under control, as otherwise it would result in side-stepping and not in a free forward sidewards moving of the horse. *Shoulder-in (l'épaule en dedans)* is the foundation of all movements on two tracks. Particular attention must be paid to the correct execution of this exercise.

In 'shoulder-in' the horse is only slightly bent in its whole length; the forehand is placed, as described, to the inside, and responding to the rider's inside leg, it steps with the inside foreleg over the outside one. The inside hindleg passes in front of the outside hindleg. The object of 'shoulder-in' is to increase the collection and the engagement of the hocks. The horse should put the inside hindleg well forward, so that the collection is adapted to the bend of its whole length.

It is essential that the horse's neck is correctly positioned on the withers. It should respond to the rider's inside leg, which acts slightly behind the girth. The neck of the horse should not be too flexed. There must be a definite position towards the inside; this should not amount to more than 45 degrees inclination, or with the forehand up to one step from the track of the outside hindleg. One should also be careful that the horse keeps its head level (not one ear lower than the other). This fault occurs from lack of suppleness in the neck and has to be corrected by work on ordinary lines, such as small circles, turns, etc. By the work in 'shoulder-in' the horse should learn to move forward with a higher degree of collection and an increased engagement of the hocks.

In the transition from the straight line to 'shoulder-in', the collection is increased by the driving aids. After half halts the rider places the forehand to the inside of the track with the inside rein which gives the horse an increased bend; the outside rein acts, together with the rider's outside leg, in a restraining way and prevents a deviating of the hindquarters to the outside. The inside leg together with the inside rein has a stronger influence and induces the horse to move forwards and sideways. By the supporting aids of the rider's back and his outside leg aids the horse will proceed in the same direction as when on one track, but in a diagonal position. The horse must maintain the *same impulsion* and the same *sequence of paces* in the movements on two tracks as in going straight on. It is important to be satisfied at the beginning with a few steps. If the horse is inclined to push against the wall, or to go back on the straight line it is advisable to turn to the inside of the arena (90 degrees).

When the horse has made sufficient progress at a walk, the rider can start with 'shoulder-in' at a collected trot. In these movements the rider should aim to support his horse—exactly as on the straight line—*equally with both reins and both legs*. It is quite obvious that sometimes the one leg or the one rein has to exert a stronger or lighter influence, dependent on the response of the horse; but it should *never* be ridden with the aid *oᵢ one leg* or *one rein only*. A horse which moves correctly in the 'shoulder-in' places the rider to the inside, is bent around his inside leg in the ribs, and is guided by the inside rein. The outside rein maintains the position and the outside leg has a *driving* and *restraining* function. The correct seat is most important. The rider should hold the upper part of his body upright and steady in the same position as in riding on one track and he must strictly avoid dropping the inside hip or twisting his shoulders. He should only support the sideways movement by slightly following with the upper part of his body the direction in which the horse is proceeding. One should furthermore pay attention to see that the impulsion is maintained. The proper sequence of the steps and the increased engagement of the hocks are most important. The horse should keep up exactly the same pace it had before on the straight line. It is therefore necessary to collect·the horse well before the transition from the straight line into the movement on two tracks, using, if necessary, increased driving aids to ensure maintaining the same rhythm and cadence, and to prevent any hesitation and irregularity of pace during the transition.

In the *Travers* (*appuyer la croupe en dedans*—quarters in, head to the wall) an increased flexion in the ribs is needed. The horse is placed in the direction to which it is moving, the sideways position being again about 30 degrees (or one pace with the quarters to the inside of the arena). The outside legs cross over the inside legs, and the horse is distinctly flexed round the rider's inside leg, except in the half pass movement (*appuyer sur la diagonale*—across the arena) where the horse should move forward, almost parallel with the track. The forehand must always be in front of the hindquarters, and at the same time a flexion to the side to which *the horse is moving* must be maintained.

In all these movements the horse must always be bent in its whole length, thus moving *forward sideways*, but it should never be pulled to the inside with the rein which would result in its hindquarters swinging to the outside.

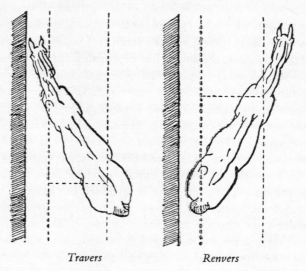

Travers   *Renvers*

Renvers (la croupe en dehors—quarters out, tail to the wall) is the opposite exercise to the *Travers* but the same rules apply as in the *Travers*, except that in the corners and turns a higher degree of training is required, as the horse has to move in a counter position.

In passing a corner at the *Travers* the hindquarters describe a shorter arc, whereas at the *Renvers* the line of the forehand is the shorter one.

In the *Travers* and *Renvers* movements the inside rein dictates the direction, the outside one the collection and the degree of deviation. The rider's inside leg maintains the stepping forward of the inside hindleg, while his outside leg prevents the swinging of the hindquarters to the outside. The influence of the inside leg and outside rein is predominant. All these movements should *not* be practised *too often*, as by too much stepping sideways the free forward movement and the proper cadence suffers. If a horse tries to push to the inside or outside, or resists the bit, the rider must correct it on a *straight* line before gradually beginning again with the movements on two tracks.

The rider must always remember that *only* a horse which is absolutely straight in its forward movements and at the same time properly balanced, is in a position to execute the movements on two tracks in a correct manner. The work on two tracks should only serve as a means to a certain purpose; thus the rider must always pay attention to maintaining the natural impulsion and a proper cadence by putting his horse straight and riding it forward.

COUNTER-CANTER (*False Canter*) AND FLYING CHANGE OF LEG (*Change in the Air*)

Every well-trained horse which will be used later on either as a dressage horse, or as a show jumper, or in the hunting field (cross-country), must be trained at the 'counter-canter' and at the 'flying change of leg'. A horse who has learned to move without difficulty at the counter-canter in a proper position and collection, and to execute the flying change of leg willingly responding to the rider's legs, will not only have great advantages in the arena as a dressage horse, but also as a show jumper and hunter through increased suppleness and obedience.

The suppleness of the dressage horse will be greatly increased by the collected counter-canter, whereby a lowering of the croup and an increased bending of the hocks will be achieved. The horse learns to obey willingly the aids of the rider, thus reaching a higher degree of obedience. Show jumpers, which are well trained at the counter-canter and execute properly the flying change of leg, are much handier when jumping a course, and they can be ridden at a fast pace even at sharp turns and short approaches. It is therefore necessary to increase the suppleness of a first class riding horse so that it is proficient in these requirements. It is obvious that one cannot expect a show jumper to be as highly collected at a shortened pace in the counter-canter and flying change of leg as a dressage horse; it should move freely forward in a bigger frame with longer extended strides.

Before starting with the 'counter-canter' the horse must be well collected and properly balanced at the shortened canter. By a turn in the corner of a long side of the arena (*demi volte*) the rider can easily execute the 'counter-canter'. The horse must, of course, be kept between the rider's seat, legs and reins. The outside rein (as at the ordinary canter) is also predominant at the counter-canter. It raises the head and keeps the horse's forehand supported by the outside leg, which prevents the horse from changing to the inside of the track. The inside leg (at the counter-canter now the outside one) maintains the canter, whereas the inside rein gives the horse—exactly as at the true canter—the direction. The corners have to be—especially at the beginning—well rounded, and the impulsion has to be increased in passing the corners, so that the horse properly learns to engage its hocks. If a horse changes leg or breaks against the rider's will, the exercise has to be repeated by a stronger influence of the outside rein and outside leg, and not by force or the use of the spur. The same applies in cantering through the corners. It is advisable to change again into the true canter by changing the rein in order to avoid the change on the track, as otherwise the horse which is not so well trained easily gets into the habit of freeing itself out of the counter-canter by a flying change. Also, here as in all other exercises, the same sequence of paces is important. At the beginning, a slight sideways position (as at the *Renvers*) may be allowed, but gradually the horse must canter in a correct head and neck position on *one* track.

The well-trained horse should change quietly and on a *straight* line at the collected and extended canter. Before one starts practising the flying change the horse has to be absolutely firm in striking off on the proper leg, and has to respond to the slightest aid of the rider's inside leg. A horse which is really light and sensitive to these inside leg-aids will not have great difficulty in learning the flying change. The rider should start with this exercise only when his horse is absolutely supple and obedient on the *straight line* and in all turns and other figures, as well as having learned to respond to the leg and rein aids. Only an *absolutely straight horse* which has reached a higher degree of collection, *without pushing sideways against the rider's legs*, is sufficiently advanced in its dressage training to be taught the correct 'flying change'. It is important that a dressage horse should *only* be taught this 'flying change' at the collected canter, whereas the show jumper and cross-country horse should not be trained at a shortened canter, but should advance with long strides in a free extended canter with longer reins and a lower head and neck position. A shortening of the neck and swinging sideways has to be avoided at all times.

The pace of the horse, cantering in proper cadence and collection, should be shortened by half halts and a simultaneous firmer grip with the legs; the horse is then ready to perform the 'flying change'. Furthermore, it is of vital importance to give the horse enough freedom at the very moment of the change, so that from the very beginning it learns to execute the change *with impulsion* in a *straight forward* direction. After the change, the horse has to be immediately brought back by half halts to the previous pace, and one has to canter on in a straight line or on a circle until it has regained its proper balance.

One should canter the horse on a big circle and execute the 'flying change' exactly at the point where one changes out of the circle, that is at the point where the peripheries of the two circles meet. Supposing the rider canters on the right rein, it is his inside leg which maintains the canter. The inside rein gives the direction, and the outside rein acts in a predominant way and dictates the diameter of the circle and the degree of collection. The outside leg is lying quietly and slightly behind the girth, supporting the influence of the inside leg; once again the inside leg and the outside rein are prevailing. Before reaching the point where he intends to change, the rider slightly shortens the pace and *increases the collection*, his legs *maintaining a good support*, in order to *increase* the engagement of the hocks, at the same time raising the horse's head and neck to such an extent that he creates a lighter contact. At this very moment the rider energetically changes the position and uses his right leg, and perhaps also the spur, in order to achieve the 'flying change'. At the moment of the change the rider should be light with his hands, thereby allowing the horse to change well forward and with impulsion. It is essential that the horse remains on a *straight line* and avoids the change by pushing sideways. Should this happen it is preferable not to change, but start again quietly. There is of course no hard and fast rule, and with many horses a different method might be advantageous.

On the big circle the 'flying change' should only be practised until the horse has learned to execute a few changes correctly. It makes it much easier if the horse is induced to execute the change at a certain point, for instance on a circle, as described. A well prepared horse will usually execute the flying change at the first attempt, and later on it will learn to do this, after repeated trials, on its own initiative. If the horse is well prepared and sufficiently advanced in its training the rider should practise the changes at a different place and not continue practising again and again on the same circle. If this is not done many horses might adopt bad habits; for instance, rushing away, or anticipating changes without the rider's command. It is of great advantage to change from a counter-canter. This can be practised on the straight line or on a big circle, depending on the suppleness and the progress the horse has made in its dressage training. If we suppose that the rider is riding on the *left rein*, he should ride on a parallel line about two paces from the track at a walk. He should then give his horse a position to the *right* and strike off about three horse lengths before the corner, the right rein and the left leg predominating. In the corner the rider should quickly and firmly change leg and rein aids; the leg aids should be applied much more strongly, in order to induce the horse to change. This changing of leg and rein aids has only to be considered as a support to the 'flying change'. It means that the right leg, which acted at the counter-canter near to the girth in a driving way, has to be energetically put back, and here support by the spurs might be advisable. The left leg on the other hand, which so far has acted in a restraining way, will be put further forward on the girth. At the same moment the horse will, of course, be placed from his position to the right into the direction to the left. It is now clear that the canter on the left rein will be continued from this moment onwards, with the inside leg on the girth (left leg) and the outside leg restraining behind the girth. The right rein will again maintain the position while the left rein directs. The exercise to teach the horse the 'flying change' by taking him back to a walk and striking off again is in my opinion not so advisable, as the horse loses much of its impulsion, and high spirited horses are easily induced to an incorrect change with a trot pace in between. I only apply this method to correct temperamental horses which anticipate the change or which push forward sideways. If a horse does not respond to the first indication, one should not force the change, but one should start again after the horse has been properly prepared. If a horse is *especially* difficult to change, then the fault lies in the fact that the horse has not yet *reached the proper stage of training*, not having learnt to respond to the leg and rein aids at an earlier stage.

The use of spurs as an aid for the flying change should be avoided, especially with well-bred horses since the reaction is disobedience and tail swishing.

JUMPING

I am only speaking here of jumping as is required of a well-trained riding horse. There are a number of very good books on the Continent and in Great Britain, which deal in detail with the training of a show jumper and cross-country horse, and it does not fall within the scope of this book to go further into this special sphere of riding.

Where there is not a jumping lane or a *couloir* at the disposal of the trainer, so that he can exercise a young horse from the beginning over very low jumps and *cavalleti*,

it is advisable to acquaint the young horse with the rudi-
ments of jumping on the lunge. Side reins should never
be used when jumping. A horse properly trained on the
lunge will quietly trot and walk on the lunge without
using side reins. Care has to be taken that the snaffle does
not slip over the horse's head; a cavesson has to be used
(as mentioned in the chapter on lunging). One should at
first put one solid bar on the ground and later on two
bars. When the horse trots very quietly over these bars
one can raise them to one and a half feet, either by using
crosses, or by putting blocks under the bars at both ends.
The young horse learns to adjust his strides and to trot
quietly and well balanced over these small jumps. The
trainer should not be rough with the lunge, and must be
very patient. Should the horse be nervous it should be
led by an assistant. One should insist on *trotting* over the
bars and small jumps and on no account allow a young
horse to canter and rush over them. The work has to be
executed equally on both reins. When the horse has made
sufficient progress on the lunge he can be ridden over the
jumps.

The trainer must take the greatest care at the beginning,
as faults and mistakes will have a bad effect on the horse's
character, and will result in bad habits and disobedience
which later on are difficult to cure without great patience.

The horse, having been taught on the lunge or in the
couloir to jump low jumps, must now learn to trot over
ground bars, *cavalleti*, and other simple jumps under the
rider. Also here, as in the whole process of dressage
training, the rider has to adjust himself to the temperament and abilities of the young horse. Very quiet work,
properly divided will lead to success. One should never
ask for too much in regard to height and the number of

jumps, and one should always endeavour to create and maintain the keenness and willingness of the youngster. Later the horse should be confronted with a variety of inviting jumps. The rider should never be sparing with praise and should reward his horse; he must always stop at the right moment, when the horse has done well, and he should only start to increase the height and spread of the jumps very gradually. By confronting a young horse with too big a jump one can easily spoil its confidence and it will be induced to refuse. Should a horse be especially nervous, for instance in jumping water, it is of great advantage for it to jump behind a leading horse. This should only be done at the beginning, as otherwise the young horse will come to expect a lead and may lose its own initiative.

To teach a horse to jump quietly and at a steady pace, the approach is most important. A young horse should always move absolutely *straight* to the middle of the jump, at a pace suitable to the type of jump, and without pushing sideways or leaning on the rider's hand. The pace should only be increased shortly before the jump. An exaggerated pace should be avoided, as the horse is then not in a position to adjust its strides and to take off at the proper point. It would quickly lose confidence and start to refuse jumps. It should learn to approach on a *straight* line and to jump right over the middle of the jump. The horse should be kept—as in dressage—between the rider's seat, legs and reins, in order to maintain a proper pace and line of approach. *A firm seat* and *steady hands* are very important! The neck of the horse should on no account be shortened. It must jump with a long neck stretched forward and downwards and well from its back, the rider holding his hands in a low, quiet position. In starting to train a young horse over jumps the rider should not dictate the take-off with his legs, or worse, with the spurs. The moment and point of take off should be left to the horse. Furthermore the rider should not try to make it easier for the horse by raising his hands, as this only interferes with the free forward movement. He should go slightly forward with his hand on the neck of the horse and give enough with the reins for the horse to execute the jump freely and quickly. This can only be achieved when it is not hindered in its back and neck; in other words, not irritated by too firm a contact and in raising its head. The rider should maintain a light even contact with the horse's mouth in all phases; in taking-off, in going over the jump, and in landing. Show jumpers and cross-country horses should not be collected and ridden in a dressage position, as this would hinder the freedom of the back (the necessary bascule). One will therefore often find horses who are very suitable for jumping or hunting, but who do not have the proper conformation to be trained as dressage horses. An unnecessary collection only irritates the horse and renders the jumping more difficult.

In jumping the rider should maintain a still, steady position and should not move about unduly in the saddle. Such movement does not help and looks ugly. At the collected canter the main support and the weight lie on the seat bones. But this is *not* the case in jumping. In jumping the rider should take a firmer grip with the knees, so that the inside part of the knees and thighs are in good contact with the saddle. The lower part of the legs maintain a steady contact with the horse's body, and the heels should be kept well down and the stirrup leathers shortened according to the rider's legs. Through this firm grip with the knees the rider will be able to unite his balance with that of his horse, adopting the so called, 'natural balanced seat'. This is the secret of the art of jumping and of training a young horse to jump willingly and with pleasure.

PART TWO

Haute École

GENERAL REMARKS CONCERNING
HAUTE ÉCOLE

AUTE ÉCOLE is the art of riding in its highest form. This art can only be achieved by systematic training on classical principles. At first the horse must be carefully and progressively trained in elementary dressage, the *'Campagne'* school, and afterwards its natural abilities can be gradually developed, until it reaches the highest stage of dressage which we call *'Haute École'*. However, only a few horses are suitable for training to this stage.

This advanced art of riding does not only consist of the different *Haute École* movements; it is the final achievement of the *'Campagne'* school, where the physical training of the horse and the development of its natural movements have reached perfection, both in its performance and in its appearance. One often hears that the practice of *Haute École* is senseless, as it does not serve any practical purpose. One can only reply by saying why do human beings practise the arts, such as music, painting, sculpture and so on? The desire and endeavour to reach complete harmony between horse and rider who must both, of course, be naturally gifted for it, by hard work and long systematic training, should be the ideal aim of every rider who intends to practise riding as an art.

If more Riding Academies existed, like the one in Vienna, the understanding of this art would be greater and more widely known. Furthermore, the oft-practised wrong methods, which lead to erroneous conceptions, would be avoided.

Haute École is unrewarding as a form of art, for after long years of training that which one has created, a horse trained to perfection, lasts only for a restricted number of years, since we are dealing with a living being.

Haute École practised on the principles of the classical art of riding should not be compared with circus riding. It is impossible for the circus rider, who is forced to train his horse in the shortest possible time, to work on classical lines and, therefore, his performances will differ greatly from the achievements of the classical *Haute École*. However, this does not mean that some circus riders do not achieve a remarkably high standard in their performances.

In the classical *Haute École*, the natural movements of the horse are developed by special exercises and by progressive training to the highest perfection. By this systematic work the horse is trained at the walk, trot and canter, up to the stage of highest collection. The horse learns to move in perfect balance, influenced by the driving and restraining aids of the rider. The natural impulsion and the exact sequence of the paces must be maintained and developed to such a degree that the rider achieves an increased cadence in all the different movements.

The *Haute École* asks for perfection, and this can only be achieved by sacrifices, consistent hard work and energy. Only after long years of arduous work will a rider emerge who looks upon riding as a creative art and who is in a position to excel in this art.

The further training of the horse which has been properly prepared in the elementary stage of dressage (called in Vienna the '*Campagne*' School) up to the more advanced standard, including the different movements of *Haute École* and its fundamental principles, will be dealt with in the second part of this book.

BALANCE
Balance is the result of impulsion in harmony with collection.

This short sentence contains everything, and the entire training of the school-horse is built upon it. The ideal aim of training is to achieve complete balance by the forward movement and the impulsion of the horse.

The method of forcing a horse by pain into collection and balance must be absolutely condemned as, by this means, complete harmony between rider and mount can never be attained.

In training the school-horse it must always be remembered that it is the primary task to achieve a rhythmical free forward movement full of impulsion, in order to develop a proper collection. A horse trained in this manner will be the ideal school-horse; it will always be possible to maintain the same high level with the help of normal aids, as the horse has attained, by systematic training of its physical abilities, a stage of training in which it moves well collected and properly balanced. The means of reaching this standard is by the development of its natural movements in connection with increased impulsion.

By this systematic building up of the natural movements in connection with an increased suppleness and a corresponding bending and positioning, the horse's muscles become stronger and more flexible. The horse which has so far only been ridden in the elementary stage of dressage with a light contact, has to be gradually improved to such an extent that it moves without pain and coercion in a proper dressage position and in perfect collection in the more advanced exercises. For this transition from elementary dressage to the requirements of the *Haute École*, a profound knowledge is necessary hand in hand with a systematic, exact programme of training in regard to what is asked from the horse. The trainer's work must be progressively planned; if one asks too much and too suddenly it will lead to a dead end, and the rider has to use force. If, on the other hand, one asks for too little over a long period, one will not achieve the necessary suppleness and obedience, resulting in a mechanized training. The trainer has to take great care to adapt the requirements and the work he asks from his horse to the progress of the individual horse. He must always adhere very carefully to the principles of elementary dressage.

A horse that has been forced into a so-called collection may, perhaps, at the beginning make quicker progress which may not, however, match his physical abilities. The horse will therefore constantly resist, and renewed force has to be applied. Apart from this, a horse which has been ridden in this manner will never be an ideal school-horse. Sometimes forcing is applied to such an extent that attempts are made in the stable to collect the horse with so-called collecting reins, in order to achieve an easier and quicker collection under the rider. This is wrong, resulting in the horse, when it moves forward, fighting the bit more than before and resisting with its head and neck. In any case, a forced collection in order to achieve a certain head carriage is to be condemned, as the action of the horse will certainly suffer.

COLLECTION AND PERFECT BALANCE

Before dealing with the training of the school-horse I should like to mention that conformation and temperament are of particular importance.

It is only natural that a well-made horse with the necessary temperament will offer less difficulty than a horse that appears to be not so suitable for High School training owing to physical shortcomings; such a horse, from the very beginning of his training, will offer more resistance to every demand.

This does not mean that a horse of faulty conformation cannot become a school-horse; on the contrary, it will become stronger and develop physically by systematic work, thereby improving in both its movements and looks. I am mentioning this so that the rider may never forget during training that all resistance on the part of the horse is more or less due to the horse's conformation and temperament. I should add that this only applies to horses which have not been spoilt as a result of faulty elementary training.

It is essential that the horse—as already described in the 'Campagne' School—should possess a good foundation before starting with a higher school collection. All the principles of training mentioned in the elementary dressage must also be adhered to in the Haute École.

A definite time at which to start with school collection for a 'campagne' horse cannot be fixed. Feeling and experience will teach the rider how quickly he can progress in the advanced training without overdoing it. The horse must be properly schooled in elementary dressage. It must have learned how to accept the bit and must move forward absolutely straight; its forelegs must definitely conform to the hindlegs, so that it executes all the different movements, turns and figures exactly on one track.

School collection is achieved by a higher degree of elevation and a simultaneous increased cadence.

The condition for this higher collection is based on the development of the hindquarters and the increased engagement of the hocks. In the period of transition from the 'Campagne' School to the stage of increased collection, the trainer has to pay the greatest attention to the proper functioning of the hindquarters. This higher collection, connected with a correct elevation, leads with increased activity of the hindlegs to a gradual transference of the centre of gravity to the rear, and teaches the horse to use his hocks more flexibly in carrying the weight of the rider. By systematic training the horse learns to move in absolute self-carriage with elastic, supple hindquarters. The achievement of perfect collection is then only a matter of time, for this is the final aim of the higher elevation. The neck rises from the withers, the nose is a little in front of the perpendicular and the poll becomes the highest point of the neck. In this way the horse moves in perfect school collection, the hindlegs come well forward, the hocks are engaged to the utmost, and the horse's back is relaxed and elastic. This perfect collection coincides with the shortened pace and results in complete balance.

The training of horses with physical shortcomings will be much more difficult. Since, unfortunately, there does not exist an ideal horse, and since it is also impossible to mention all the different faults of conformation with the corresponding variations of training which they demand, I must content myself in saying that only experience can help the school-rider here. No definite rules can be laid down with regard to the work on a living being; each rider must gain his experience on each horse.

With all horses the development of the natural movements is the primary factor. It is mainly at the trot that one has to train the horse, so that it learns to react correctly to the rider's leg and rein aids and to carry itself in the necessary balance and collection.

The better the horse is trained at the trot, the easier will it find the other tasks. In trotting it is important, at the outset, that the horse is not worked at too collected a school trot. It must be ridden at a somewhat more extended pace, so that it learns to use its hindquarters; it will also be easier to achieve at this pace a higher collection.

In the case of horses which are inclined to seek a support from the rider's hand in higher collection, the increased elevation must only be gradually asked for and the pace should not be suddenly shortened.

Furthermore, if such horses have a short, very strong back, they must be ridden in a position in which the nose is slightly in front of the perpendicular. In this way the horse will gradually relax the muscles in its back, and this makes it unnecessary for it to seek support from the reins, and it gradually learns to move in self carriage. This is the first aim which should be achieved and perfected. The relation between elevation and movement which I mentioned before is meant in the sense that the elevation should never impede the proper following up of the hindlegs and the urge to move freely forward. A horse trained on these principles will always respond properly to the leg and rein aids, as the elevation makes it impossible to resist in its back. In my opinion, the horse's main source of resistance lies in its back. All other ways of resisting are more or less connected with it. I therefore think it is most important that from the beginning of its training the horse learns to relax and to become supple in its back. In this way it should move in all figures and turns, so that it can execute them without resistance at any desired pace. In order to achieve this it is essential that the rider acts with a firm, quiet seat and a braced back. The hands, supported by the upper arms, are kept quiet and steady in order to correct the horse by corresponding driving and rein aids in case it shows resistance by leaning on the bit. It is essential to hold the hands in a very still position. Rein aids acting backwards must be avoided, and *arrêts* are only allowed in exceptional cases in order to achieve the required elevation. It is most important to avoid any collecting rein aids, as the proper engagement of the hindlegs and the impulsion would suffer. The horse should respond to the light leg aids in order to execute willingly what is asked from it by its rider. It is an erroneous opinion that one can maintain the impulsion by continuous strong leg aids or by flapping with the legs. It entirely depends on the proper application of the aids to maintain the horse's sensitiveness. Each leg aid should be lightly applied with an even contact. If the horse does not react willingly and quickly the aid must be immediately applied strongly and energetically, so that later it responds to the subsequent light aids. It must be again and again pointed out that the rider has to act with a firm, quiet seat. The firmer the seat, the more effective is the aid, as an unsteady seat distracts the horse's attention and its sensitiveness suffers. Quiet, evenly applied leg aids are necessary for regular paces and the relaxation of the horse.

As previously mentioned, the horse has to be ridden in a position in which it is induced to relax in its back. The expression, 'to relax in its back', signifies that the relaxing point lies behind the withers. This is also the point on which the rein aids exercise their influence by the action of the rider's back. If a horse relaxes because of an excessive elevation, the suppleness of the back and the engagement of the hindlegs would suffer. It is therefore important that the elevation always corresponds with the pace, and that the hocks are well engaged. Accordingly, a proper relationship must exist between the driving and

PLATE XI. *Interior of the Spanish Riding School, Vienna*

PLATE XII. *Von Adlerkreutz (Sweden) on "Teresina" and the Author on "Burgsdorff."*
Joint winners Olympic Dressage Test, Aachen, 1935

PLATE XIII. *Extended Trot. The Olympic horse Malteser* (1964)

PLATE XIV. *Lindenbauer (Vienna) Pirouette Left*

Pirouette Left   PLATE XV.   *Pirouette Right*

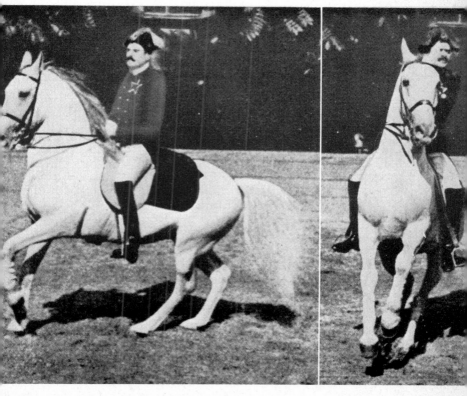

PLATE XVI. *Meixner (Vienna) Pirouette Left*

PLATE XVII. (*left*). *Canter counter-change* (*Traversale*) *to the left.*
(*right*). *Canter-counter-change* (*Traversale*) *to the right.*

PLATE XVIII. *The Author teaching the horse the Piaffe on the ground*

PLATE XIX. *Lt. Colonel Handler (Director of the Spanish Riding School, Vienna) on Siglavy Bona demonstrating the Piaffe. Exemplary movement executed on the spot in complete collection with Classically ideal style*

PLATE XX. *Colonel Podhajsky, Commandant of the Spanish Riding School on* "Neapolitano Africa" *at the Piaffe, in beautifully executed, perfect harmony*

PLATE XXI. *The Author at the Piaffe*

PLATE XXII. *The Author at the Piaffe (Historical Quadrille)*

PLATE XXIII. *Piaffe in the Pillars*

PLATE XXIV. *The author riding the 7-year-old black gelding "Christian"
executing the Piaffe* (1957)

restraining aids, which have to be applied in such a way that the horse is influenced to maintain the proper sequence of the paces and the necessary impulsion. In this elevating task it is important that the rein aids act in the direction of the centre of the rider's body, for only in this way is it possible to act upon the horse's back by the influence of the rider's back. This shows that the rein aids act more in an elevating than in a collecting way. Collecting rein aids must be strictly avoided. The head and neck carriage must always be in harmony with the horse's impulsion.

In this first stage the horse has to be schooled on these lines, so that it can execute in a proper cadence and with an even contact all the different movements, turns and other figures required by the rider.

In order to achieve perfect collection the rider should gradually aim to train his horse at shorter paces in a so-called 'school' position. It is very important that the vertical head position should not be achieved by force, but should be the result of the preceding work. The horse should not be pulled into this position, but should be driven into it. The perfect collection should be achieved by the rhythm of the pace, the impulsion and the light contact with the horse's mouth.

It depends, of course, on the individual horse how much one can ask in this direction. The perfect collection can only be gradually achieved as, by excessive and too early collection, the free forward movement would suffer and the horse would resist by going sideways and stiffening its back. The rider's hand must be absolutely still and steady with a supple wrist, as a restless hand in no way furthers the collection. On the contrary, the unsteady contact irritates the horse and it ceases to be sensitive to the proper rein aids. I again wish to emphasize that when a horse has learned to move in a proper school collection achieved by progressive, systematic work, this position can always be maintained by the rider's normal influences.

In the case of high-spirited horses with weak backs and lacking impulsion one should ride them at first with the hands in a fairly low position, and one should only attempt a higher collection in accordance with an increased engagement of the hindlegs. The rider should make himself as light as possible, and the shortening of the pace should only be demanded in accordance with the increased collection.

The proper distribution of work is of great importance. The rider must know instinctively how much he can ask from his horse. In schooling the rider should not be misled into working his horse too much in movements on two tracks and for too long a period at shortened paces, otherwise the desired proper cadence and the impulsion would suffer.

THE SCHOOL WALK

The school walk is a pace of the High School to which generally too little importance is attached, for it is possible to attain by the work at the walk a high level of training for the horse. A horse that carries out all the figures, turns and lateral work at a correct walk will be well prepared for the work at the trot and the canter. It learns to respond to the leg and rein aids and to maintain its balance at the school walk. Furthermore, the walk must be regarded as a means of correction, as many of the horse's shortcomings can only be corrected at the walk. For this reason great care should be taken with the walk, and it should be regarded in no way as an unimportant pace.

In the school walk the horse should be perfectly collected and move in a proper dressage position. The poll must be the highest point of the neck and the head must adopt a vertical position. This ideal carriage depends on the individual qualities and the conformation of the horse. It should not be continually required from it, but should be practised for shorter or longer periods according to the ability of the horse.

The walk of the *campagne* horse should consist of long, even strides, gaining much ground, whereas the school horse walks with shorter, more elevated steps. In order to ask for a school walk the horse must have been trained very thoroughly in elementary dressage, as the pace would suffer if the school walk is practised too soon. In order to change from the *campagne* walk into the school walk the desired higher carriage has to be achieved by increased driving aids of the legs and corresponding restraining rein aids. A well trained *campagne* horse which responds properly to the rider's aids and is supple, will not offer any particular difficulty. As already mentioned, the periods of the school walk should be short and it is advisable to practise it as a transition to a more extended pace. For a horse that is well on the bit at the collected school walk and is light and supple, it will not be difficult to maintain the proper carriage in the transition to a more extended pace, without resistance and with a light contact. Gradually, the rider should aim at riding his horse at the school walk for longer periods. The regularity of the pace is most important, as this is one of the main principles of schooling, and without it a steady head carriage and an even, light contact cannot be achieved.

It is, of course, difficult to deal with the correction of faults at a walk. I only want to point out that the rider has to pay the greatest attention to the regularity of the pace and the exact sequence of the strides. The aids applied by the rider must never interfere with the proper rhythm and cadence.

With horses that are inclined to be behind the bit one should not attempt a school collection at too early a stage. Such horses should be ridden freely forward and worked at an extended walk with a long rein.

Great care should be taken with the lateral work at the walk. As said earlier, the work at the walk is a good preparation for the corresponding work at the trot, and facilitates it. Great exactness is required. The horse must proceed straight on one track in a correct head carriage and position, maintaining the same pace with regular, even strides. Any side stepping has to be strictly avoided. The hoofs of the hindlegs should step exactly in the tracks of the forelegs. If the horse steps shorter with one hindleg the collection should be decreased and the walk extended until the correct sequence of the pace is re-established. Only quite gradually should the rider begin again with a higher collection and correspondingly shorten the stride. In the lateral work at the school walk the rider has to be very careful to maintain the fluency of the movement in the transition from the straight line to the lateral position, avoiding any hesitation and interruption of the proper cadence. The school horse should execute these move-ments with elevated steps, in perfect collection and rhythm. The tracks of the fore and hindlegs are parallel to each other. The horse is bent in its whole length and this position should be clearly noticeable.

It is of the greatest importance for the *campagne* horse, and for the school horse as well, that the rider is in a position to execute at any time with smooth transitions, an even, extended walk, as well as a free walk on the long rein. A true, exact, cadenced walk has still more to be taken into consideration than in the past. I should like to quote a great expert, the late Dr. G. Rau, who said, 'If a horse does not make progress in the walk in its dressage work, the whole system of training has been wrong. The walk in its different phases must continually improve. This is the proof of a sound dressage training on correct principles.'

THE SCHOOL TROT

The school trot is the most important movement. It is the foundation for all other movements. In the training at the school trot the rider has to take the greatest care in regard to a correct pace, suppleness, lightness and a proper position. Whereas in the *'campagne'* school (the elementary dressage) the horse moves freely forward with long even strides, at the school trot the horse gains less ground and moves with a higher degree of collection. The steps must be rhythmical and lively, the impulsion be more upward than forward, resulting in an exact cadence, and the engagement of the hocks being increased to the utmost. Dragging passage-like steps are a sign of tension and are a bad fault. The horse should move in perfect collection. In the elevation of head and neck the point of the nose is approximately in a line with the hip, and the nose itself slightly in front of the vertical, otherwise the impulsion and the elastic action of the horse's back suffers.

In the training at the school trot the same principles apply as in the elementary dressage. These are described in the chapter 'Balance'. Accordingly, the proper sequence of the paces, self carriage and suppleness are most important. At the beginning, the transition from the ordinary trot to the school trot in a higher collection should only be practised for short periods and then quite gradually prolonged. One should always maintain the liveliness of the pace in changing from the collected trot to the ordinary and extended trot. One achieves increased suppleness by the transition to the movements on two tracks. The horse has to learn systematically to move at an even, cadenced pace, in a proper position and flexion, at the command of its rider.

WORK ON TWO TRACKS

The object of the work on two tracks is to increase the horse's obedience and suppleness in all its paces, and to achieve, by correct schooling, lightness and perfect balance.

'Shoulder-in' is the foundation of all lateral work. I have already described the principles in the first part of this book. Far higher demands are asked from a school horse. The movement has to be carried out in a higher collection and with an increased bend in its whole length. The most important point is that the horse maintains the correct pure school trot. Particular attention must, therefore, be paid to the horse only being bent to such an extent that it can still execute the trot in a proper rhythm in the required diagonal position. By systematic training the rider must achieve a state where his horse moves in the correct lateral position. As previously mentioned, this work must be entirely adapted to the abilities of the horse and should not be practised either too often or for too long a period. The horse should move as well in lateral work as at the school trot, being supported by the light leg and rein aids of the rider. It should lean neither to the inside nor to the outside. At the shoulder-in it is the inside rein which leads the horse to the inside and gives the direction; the outside rein restrains and dictates the degree of the sidewards position. The inside leg drives the horse, bent in its whole length, forward, and the outside leg, kept slightly behind the girth, supports the forward movement in a restraining manner. These aids have to be adapted to the reaction of the particular horse in order to achieve the ideal contact with legs and reins. In this exercise it is very important, especially when riding in the corners, that the horse always moves at the same angle and in the same sideways position. If the horse has been equally trained on both reins in the shoulder-in the foundation is laid for all other movements on two tracks. The condition, of course, is that the horse moves absolutely straight and correctly on one track before

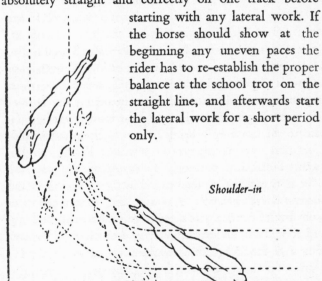

starting with any lateral work. If the horse should show at the beginning any uneven paces the rider has to re-establish the proper balance at the school trot on the straight line, and afterwards start the lateral work for a short period only.

Shoulder-in

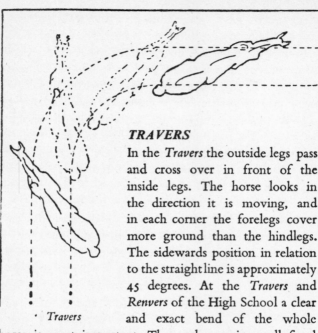

Travers

TRAVERS

In the *Travers* the outside legs pass and cross over in front of the inside legs. The horse looks in the direction it is moving, and in each corner the forelegs cover more ground than the hindlegs. The sidewards position in relation to the straight line is approximately 45 degrees. At the *Travers* and *Renvers* of the High School a clear and exact bend of the whole horse is most important. The neck remains well fixed at the withers and should not be more bent than the horse in its whole curvature. *Travers* and *Renvers* ought only to be ridden for short periods, as it is quite strenuous for the horse to move in a highly collected position with an increased bend. The rhythmical, cadenced school trot must be maintained with a clear forward-sideward impulse, the pace being the same as on one track. In the work on two tracks, the rein and leg aids act in a diagonal way and an even, light contact with the horse's mouth is most important.

RENVERS

Renvers is the counter-exercise to *Travers*, with the tail instead of the head to the wall. The degree of the bend and the position, and the head and neck carriage are similar to those of *Travers*. It is the inverse position of the *Travers*. The horse is also looking in the direction in which it is moving, the difference being that in the corners, the hindlegs cover more ground than the forelegs. What has been said about leg and rein aids in connection with *Travers* applies also to *Renvers*. I want to emphasize again that these exercises have to be adjusted to the stage the horse has reached in its schooling. If a horse shows any resistance in *Travers* and *Renvers*—for instance in resisting with head and neck—it must not be corrected in these exercises, but by changing to shoulder-in. One should always remember that the horse must be chiefly worked on a straight line, i.e., on one track, for excessive schooling in lateral work causes even the most accomplished horse to lose its impulsion. If a horse tries to evade, either by shortening his stride or by breaking into a canter, one should not bring it back to a walk and collect it, but instead drive it on into a shoulder-in position until it moves in a proper school trot and executes the desired lateral work with corresponding contact of the rider's leg. Particular attention should be paid to the correct position of the neck, which should not be bent from the withers to the poll, but correspond to the bend of the horse in its whole length, i.e., bent in the ribs around the rider's inside leg. In the higher school work a greater bend is, of course, asked for than in the '*campagne*' school. Furthermore, the rider must be very careful always to sit in a correct position, the upper part of the body upright, and not hanging to one side or dropping the inside hip. He must always follow the movement of the horse, keeping his shoulders parallel to the horse's shoulders.

In considering the work on two tracks I now want to mention the traverse movements to the right and left: the half pass diagonally across the arena and the counter change of hands. In the more advanced tests (*Grand Prix de Dressage*) the rider has to execute a certain number of steps to the right and left (zig-zag movement). These exercises, correctly executed, comprise one of the most difficult movements at the school trot and require absolute looseness and suppleness of the horse.

The rider must be careful that his horse moves freely forward on two tracks, the head, neck and shoulders always slightly in advance of the quarters. The horse is only slightly bent, looking in the direction of the movement, and its position is almost parallel to the straight line. It is a sign of a well-trained school horse if it quickly changes from the right to the left, always slightly bent in its ribs, and maintaining a lively cadenced school trot. The rider's inside leg creates the correct bend and the forward movement, while his outside leg influences the horse to step to the right or left. The change from the one side to the other and the corresponding bend has to be very exactly executed. If the horse loses its cadence and impulsion in these lateral exercises one should not continue with them by trying to correct the horse by force. One should at first ride freely forward on a straight line and then start with corresponding exercises in *Travers* and *Renvers*.

EXTENDED TROT

It should be borne in mind that the school horse must always remain a useful '*campagne*' horse. For this reason, the extended trot and the very extended trot must not be neglected. For a well-trained horse the smooth transition from the school trot to the extended trot will not offer any difficulty. It is the proof of its proper schooling. Furthermore, these extended movements increase the impulsion and the engagement of the hocks, and this will be of invaluable help in the shortened school paces.

SCHOOL CANTER

The careful development of the school canter is of the greatest importance and the foundation of all other exercises at the highly collected canter.

Like the school trot the school canter, as compared with the canter in the *'campagne'* school, is not a free forward movement gaining much ground. The horse must take short elevated strides and this will, of course, be connected with an increased elevation and collection and a corresponding engagement of the hindlegs. The proper cadence plays a great part at the school canter; it must be regular, no matter how short the horse is asked to canter. The impulsion must be maintained to such an extent that the natural stride and the correct sequence of the pace do not suffer. Naturally, the school canter must be developed, like the school trot, from the collected canter by an increased elevation and collection and a simultaneous greater engagement of the hocks, so that the strides become shorter and more elevated. It depends, of course, on the individual horse how quickly the rider can proceed with this work. A well-made horse will not experience any difficulty in maintaining the school canter for shorter or longer periods. The canter, however, should only be shortened to such an extent that the horse does not deviate from the straight line with its hindlegs and lose its impulsion through the resultant uneven strides.

In this case the horse should not be forced into a collected school canter, but the pace must be increased until it has regained its impulsion and once again proceeds absolutely straight on one track. Afterwards the rider should start again with the school canter. The hands of the rider must be kept in a perfectly still, steady position. The rider should not try to support the canter with rein aids. On the contrary, in going with the movement, he should release every stride. The periods of the school canter entirely depend on the horse's abilities; they must be so arranged that through successive training the horse learns to maintain this collected school canter for longer periods.

The correct striking off to a school canter is of the greatest importance. The horse should be so well trained that it strikes off to the desired highly collected canter at the slightest indication from the rider, without deviating with the hindquarters from the straight line. It is therefore necessary to collect the horse and to prepare it for the smooth striking-off. How this is done depends on the horse's temperament. With a lazy, sluggish horse a short, energetic aid with the inside leg—in some cases supported with the spur—might be necessary. The horse should strike off on a straight line. Both legs must act in a way which makes a deviation from the track impossible. The canter should be created after a proper collection with a very light influence of the inside leg. In the strike off the rider's hands must remain quiet and still. Both reins act in an elevating way which induces the horse to strike off at the school canter, highly collected and well elevated. To maintain the school canter and the proper impulsion the influence of the rider's inside leg is predominant, whereas his outside leg keeps the horse on the straight line and prevents the swinging of the quarters to the outside in corners and circles. The correction for breaking into a trot is different. With a lazy horse which is able to maintain the collected school canter, but which does not respond sufficiently to the light aids of the leg, one has to re-establish the canter with a short, energetic aid. With a high-spirited horse, however, which avoids the collected movement by rushing forward, one has to strike off again in a very quiet way and then gradually shorten the pace with great patience in order to achieve the desired school canter. It is wrong if the rider tries to maintain the short collected pace by continuous rein and weight aids. In the school canter the influence of the rider's back and the balance of driving and restraining aids play a major part.

HALF AND FULL HALTS

The half and full halts are of the greatest help for the rider in training the school horse. By diligent and correct practice of these halts the horse becomes supple and pliable in the hocks. It learns to shorten the pace and to change the centre of gravity at the rider's indication.

The school horse should execute the half halt in the transition to the walk with supple, well-engaged hocks. The pace should be gradually shortened, so that the last stride takes place almost on the spot, the horse then changing into the walk without any hesitation. As when striking off to the canter, attention should be paid to the proper head carriage and elevation. Therefore, horses which are inclined to rush in executing the halts, must be accordingly elevated, whereas horses which hesitate should be less collected, and special attention must be paid to the engagement of the hindlegs. Like all other exercises, the halts should be systematically practised and should not be required too often, as a young horse gets tired through excessive practice of halts, becomes insensitive to the aids, and will suffer in its hocks. In the work at the canter the halts are of the greatest importance, as a horse which executes the halts correctly is able to maintain the short, collected school canter without any effort, almost on the spot. The half and full halts are also a good preparation for the Pirouettes and all other short turns and figures at the canter.

THE PIROUETTE

The Pirouette is the turn on the haunches in five to six strides at a collected canter. The horse, with its hocks well engaged, does the turn with its hindlegs completing the smallest possible circle, almost on one spot, and with the forelegs describing a wider circle round the hindlegs. The correct cadence and proper sequence of the strides must be maintained. The Pirouette is one of the most difficult exercises of the *Haute École*, as a correct execution demands a perfectly trained horse, accurately responding to the rider's aids. Of a well trained '*campagne*' horse one should not ask more than an about-turn at the canter, as for the proper execution of the Pirouette a greatly increased engagement of the hocks and a more collected, elevated, canter are essential; these cannot be expected from a '*campagne*' horse.

There are two ways in which to teach the horse the Pirouette, either on a straight line, i.e., on a single track, practising a double about-turn, or from the *Renvers* position in the corner of the school with three-quarter Pirouettes.

It is far more difficult to teach the horse the Pirouette by practising a double about-turn, and I do not think it is advisable. The horse easily learns to throw the quarters around, getting behind the bit, deviating with the hind-legs and losing the proper cadence. Only when a horse has gained a certain experience in the three-quarter Pirouettes can one start with the double-turn.

Before attempting the Pirouette the horse must canter quietly in perfect collection, with short, elevated strides. The striking-off and the half halts are of the greatest importance for the Pirouette. The horse has to strike off at the slightest indication from the rider, and be able to shorten the pace well collected. The striking-off must be well established on the influence of the rider's inside leg, in order to maintain and, if necessary, re-start the canter. The horse must be able to execute a smooth and collected halt from the canter. This enables him to acquire the suppleness necessary to shorten the pace before the Pirouette and, with elevated strides and well engaged hocks, to execute the Pirouette with full impulsion on a very small circle. By a turn-about at the canter the rider leads his horse into a *Renvers* canter.

Shortly before the corner one rides a *volte* (small circle of about 6 yards diameter) to the outside, keeping the quarters with the outside leg in a *Travers*-like way to the inside. The *volte* at the beginning should be large enough to maintain the canter without hesitation, in order to be able to progress afterwards on a line parallel to the wall. The diameter of the circle depends on the suppleness of the horse and on the distance of the parallel line from the wall (page 87).

It cannot be over-emphasized that the rider should endeavour to guide his horse exactly on the indicated line, as it is only possible in this way to establish absolute obedience. The whole essence of dressage actually consists of riding the horse on the proper lines at the required pace and exact cadence.

If the horse canters in a *Renvers* canter on the right rein parallel to the wall the rider should keep his horse exactly on this line. Any pushing to the inside or to the outside has to be strictly avoided. If necessary, in order to correct a fault, one has to bring the horse back to the walk, take it to the proper line and strike off again. In the *Renvers* canter the right rein and the left leg are predominant: the right rein regulating the position, the

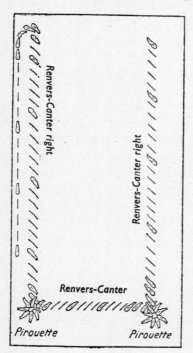

Renvers-Canter right

Renvers-Canter right

Renvers-Canter

Pirouette   Pirouette

left leg, kept still and restricting, preventing the falling-out of the quarters in the Pirouette. The right leg maintains the lively stride, and the outside left rein restrains and elevates, thus preventing a pushing towards the wall. The rider must avoid pulling his horse with both reins to the side in the *Renvers* canter. The hands must remain in front of and in the middle of the rider's body and the rein aids must act in the direction of the body. In other words, the horse must be 'guided' by the rider in the true sense of the word. Furthermore, the rider should endeavour to sit still and upright, in order not to disturb the canter by shifting his body about and by applying weight aids. The more still the rider sits, the better the horse will respond to his aids.

Before starting the Pirouette the horse must be well elevated by the driving aids of both legs, mainly the inside one, to bring the hindlegs well forward and to guide the horse into the proper movement, which should not be considered as anything but a small *volte*. The horse must execute this *volte* in a *Travers* position with elevated strides and a lowered croup. The right rein regulates the position, and the right leg maintains the canter and the impulsion; the left rein dictates the diameter of the circle and the left leg prevents the hindquarters from falling out. After the exercise is finished the horse must again be guided to the parallel line. If the horse is sufficiently prepared it will execute this figure without difficulty. In the Pirouette itself the same pace must be maintained as on the straight line. If the horse has easily executed the first three-quarter Pirouette, the same exercise can be attempted in the next corner. Otherwise one should just canter through the corner, and after a transition to the walk, continue the Pirouette at this pace. The first exercises should not be practised too often. When the horse has reached the stage where it can execute the above figures with absolute obedience, one can gradually decrease the circles according to the ability of the horse. The rider must keep the hindquarters more to the inside, so that the horse moves around in a lateral position (on two tracks) in order, eventually, to achieve in this way the three-quarter Pirouette. In decreasing the circle and giving the horse the sideways

Travers position, one has to be careful that the horse does not rush around trying to execute the Pirouette of its own accord at an exaggerated pace. In this case, the outside rein acting towards the body has to prevent the independent turning of the horse. If a restraining influence is not enough to correct the faults, one has to bring the horse back to a walk at the very moment when it starts to rush around. Here again, the outside rein and the inside leg are predominant in such a way that the outside rein pulls the horse up without altering the position, in order to continue the exercise at a quiet walk. On reaching the straight line, one should again strike off at a canter, in order to start the same exercise in the next corner. If one has corrected the horse several times in this way, one can again strike off in the Pirouette, in order to continue the second part of the Pirouette. In this way the horse will learn to respond exactly to the leg and rein aids. By his skill and experience, the rider will grasp the exact moment when the horse starts to rush and throw itself around, and he will correct it. But this can only be achieved if the rider sits in an absolutely still, steady position. If, on the other hand, the horse hesitates in the Pirouette, then it has to be driven forward with both legs; the pace has to be increased and a bigger circle has to be ridden; in this case the rider must be prepared to drive his horse with impulsion to the bit and then, quite gradually, to decrease the three-quarter Pirouette. In this way the horse learns to execute the Pirouette in a quiet even pace with the proper sequence of the strides.

The school horse should perform the Pirouette from the *Renvers* canter in such a way that both tracks remain parallel to each other up to the last moment, and this should also be the case after the Pirouette is finished. The horse should not seek any support from the reins in the Pirouette, which must be executed with a light contact. But to achieve this, a perfect collection and proper elevation are necessary. Before the Pirouette the horse should be animated to short, lively and cadenced strides, in order to create the necessary elevation corresponding to the short turn, and it should not show any resistance in its back. The hand has to be kept in an absolutely still position. It does not help in any way to animate the horse with rein aids and *arrêts* if it loses its impulsion in the Pirouette. The rider must go back on a straight line and drive the horse with the legs into a lively canter. Afterwards, if necessary, he should begin the exercise again on a bigger circle. In order to render the horse supple and obedient in the Pirouettes, it is advisable to revert frequently to a walk and then to strike off afresh at a canter. In these exercises the horse must be very sensitive to the rein and leg aids, and respond to the slightest indication of the rider. Only in this way is it possible for the horse to execute the short turn, supported by the rider's invisible aids, in a correct and pleasing manner. Special attention must be paid to ensure that the horse does not hurry in the Pirouettes, and is not thrown around, but maintains the same even, rhythmical stride. It takes quite a long time and diligent, systematic work before the horse is in a position to execute correct and cadenced Pirouettes. Especially difficult are the full Pirouettes, which have to be ridden on a straight line and on one track; for instance, on the diagonal, in the advanced Olympic test (Grand Prix de Dressage).

THE 'FLYING CHANGE OF LEG' AT THE CANTER

In the first part of the book the 'flying change' of leg of a well trained '*campagne*' horse has already been discussed in detail. Here we are dealing with the changes of leg of a school horse and their execution at a certain number of strides.

The difference of the 'flying change' as asked from a '*campagne*' horse and a school horse must be made clear. The '*campagne*' one—executed if necessary at a fairly free pace—should be a free forward movement, gaining ground with impulsion, but with not much collection. In contrast to this the school horse is asked to change in the air with a much increased engagement of the hocks, in perfect collection at the school canter. This requires a considerably greater suppleness of the horse, as it has to change with impulsion without altering the pace, while remaining exactly on one track, but with a different position and bend. The school horse which canters accurately and lightly in circles and turns, is now schooled in the 'flying change of leg' in certain exercises, like figures-of-eight and changes through the circle. If the horse is firm in these exercises one can start the changes at a certain number of strides. Before discussing this in detail I want to mention that I have seen horses, even at big shows, which change at every fourth stride and even less, without any engagement of the hocks and proper collection. This does not conform to the principles of the classical art of riding. In the Olympic *Grand Prix de Dressage* the flying changes are highly valued, and their correct execution is a proof of the properly schooled dressage horse. When the horse is asked for the change of leg at a certain number of strides he has to execute it with impulsion from the hindlegs to the front and on an exactly straight line.

It is not advisable to practise the changes on the long track next to the wall of the school; inside the school the rider has a better control over his horse. It depends on the horse's temperament and ability as to the number of strides between each change when starting this movement. A well-schooled horse which has the right temperament will be able to perform the change after each fifth or sixth stride. When it has learned to do this, one can start with the changes at every four, three and, finally, two strides. In these exercises it frequently happens that horses anticipate the rider's aids by changing too early. This must be immediately checked, for the horse must only change at the very moment when the aid is given. This anticipation leads later on to a resistance by which the horse evades the aids. Correction of the too-early change entirely depends on the individual behaviour of the horse. Horses which are inclined to rush forward must be corrected by being checked at the very moment of the faulty change, and then quickly brought back to the original lead. The horse should then be cantered on this lead until it canters quietly, without attempting to change on its own accord. Only then should the rider again start with the 'flying changes'. Horses which hesitate, when asked to change, must be brought back to the original lead by energetic leg aids and kept to this lead until they canter quietly without trying to change. The leg aids must be applied in maintaining contact with the horse's side, as only in this way is it possible to keep the horse on a straight line. These leg aids must be adapted to the sensitiveness of the individual horse and they naturally vary. It depends on the sensitivity and skill of the rider to apply the aids at the right moment and with the necessary vigour. It is essential that the rider keeps up the contact with both legs, only changing the position according to the change. For horses which do not properly respond, short and energetic leg aids are necessary. In the 'flying change' the bend must be accordingly changed, and harmony must always exist between rein and leg aids. The rider has to take great care to change the bend as quietly as possible. The horse must not be thrown with the reins from one side to the other. Furthermore, the rider has to create the necessary collection and elevation in which it is possible for the horse to change smoothly and with impulsion. An excessive collection would render the task more difficult and weaken the hindlegs.

In the change in the air the seat of the rider plays an important part. He must keep the upper part of his body straight and steady. It is in no way necessary to assist the change by so-called weight aids; the rider has only to follow the movement.

Only when the horse is quite firm in the change at every two strides can the rider attempt the change at every stride. He has to apply the same aids as in the two-stride change, but he must pay great attention to ensuring that the aids are given quickly enough and following each other with exact precision. If the rider is not able to follow the strides of his horse he will apply the aids too late, with the result that he will be against, instead of with the movement of the horse. When changing at every stride the horse must be allowed, especially at the beginning, to move forward sufficiently to execute the change with impulsion and on a straight line. To start with the rider must be content with two or three changes, before gradually demanding more. Not until the horse has learned to change correctly at a somewhat quicker pace, should the rider attempt the change at every stride in a higher collection and at a shorter pace.

THE PIAFFE

The *Piaffe* is the trot on the spot (*le trot sur place*). The horse steps diagonally in perfect regularity and good cadence, with hocks well engaged. The centre of gravity rests entirely on the hocks, which receive the weight in an elastic, springy way. The impulsion is directed upwards instead of forwards. The *Piaffe* is an *Haute École* movement which requires absolute obedience, perfect suppleness and lightness. A long systematic training with great experience and knowledge on the part of the rider is necessary for a smooth cadenced *Piaffe*. It is the foundation of all movements of the classical school 'on and above the ground'. Only the *Piaffe*, which has been developed by correct, methodical and gymnastic work, will make a harmonious, pleasing impression, executed by the horse without effort. Horses which have been schooled by force, resulting in pain for the animal, show a cramped, tensed action.

The *Piaffe* of the classical school differs from the 'circus *Piaffe*' or '*Piaffe* balancé', in which the horse deviates at each stride to the left and right with unbent hocks. The execution of the *Piaffe* partly depends on the conformation of the horse. For this reason the degree, to which the hindlegs can be brought under the body, varies.

There are several methods of teaching the horse the *Piaffe*. It can be taught under the rider by the influence of the legs and whip, and also from the ground. The most advantageous method is from the ground, without the horse being burdened by the weight of the rider. In this way it learns more easily to engage and bend the hocks and to bring the hindlegs well forward. In contrast to the work in the pillars the horse may be allowed, when performing the *Piaffe* from the ground, to advance a little to make it easier at the beginning. For work from the ground one should use side reins. A cavesson is used, to which a leading rein is attached, which should act in the same way as the rider's reins. A horse being worked from the ground is kept between the leading rein and the whip, in exactly the same way as between the reins and legs when being ridden. A horse that has learned to perform the *Piaffe* from the ground willingly and obediently, can easily be placed in the pillars, and will, within a very short time, execute the *Piaffe* without great difficulty. When working from the ground, the side reins must be fixed in such a way that the head and nose of the horse when in motion are almost vertical, exactly as in work on the lunge. This gives the rider more control over his mount, and the horse learns at the same time to execute the *Piaffe* with a correct head carriage. The side reins should not be too short, as this prevents the proper engagement of the hocks and the following-up of the hindlegs, and might lead to resistance. It is essential that the horse should be well acquainted with the work on the lunge.

To simplify the description of *Piaffe* work from the ground let us assume that we commence this exercise on the left rein. With a cavesson and properly adjusted side reins, the horse is led to the wall of the manège. The leading rein is held fairly short in the left hand, the rider standing approximately on a level with the horse's shoulders, and the whip is held in the right hand. With the whip, gently applied to the hindlegs, one induces the horse to step forward, and by simultaneous restraining aids of the leading rein, the horse is kept back. Through frequent repetition of these exercises the horse will make a few elevated steps at the trot. The whip and the leading rein aids must have the same influence as the leg and rein aids when ridden, and must be adapted to the reactions of the horse. It varies how much one allows the horse to step forward in this exercise. It must never be restrained to such an extent that the hindquarters deviate from the track, for if the horse has once learned this means of resistance it is very difficult to correct it. In such a case one should drive the horse forward, and, if necessary, forego the *Piaffe* exercise altogether, and only require it to advance in a short trot in response to the aid of the whip, keeping it on the track by leading the fore-legs slightly to the inside in a shoulder-in position.

It is very important to practise this exercise for short periods only, the rider being satisfied at the beginning with one or two steps. The rider must not forget that for some horses the increased bending of the hocks is very difficult, and resistance in most cases is the result of asking too much from the horse. The rider will succeed far better in this exercise by regular, slow, systematic work. In the first lessons one should not practise for more than four or five minutes, so that the horse never starts to resist. The whip aids should be short, energetic and applied in such a manner that the horse never kicks against the whip or resents it. The aids of the leading rein act in the same way as the rein aids, and should be used as when mounted, maintaining an even light contact with the horse's mouth. If an increased contact does not suffice to keep the horse back in the *Piaffe* exercise, it is necessary to re-establish the desired position by one or two short, energetic *arrêts*. In the case of excitable horses it is advisable in the pre-liminary stage to support the aid of the leading rein by the use of the inside snaffle rein. It entirely depends on the skill of the trainer not to drive the horse so much that it leans on the guiding rein. Here, as when mounted, harmony must exist between whip and rein aids. The *arrêts* given by the leading rein should not be given too often, otherwise a quiet contact cannot be established, and the horse will suffer in its paces. The restraining aids must never interfere with the lively steps of the hindlegs. If it happens that the hindlegs come to a standstill by too much restraint, the horse must be driven well forward with the aid of the whip and induced to use its hindlegs in the desired way. It is advisable to practise the *Piaffe* on the same rein until the horse is quite obedient and has made good progress, as a too early change of rein would delay the work. As already mentioned, it is advisable to start the exercise on the left rein, as one usually leads the horse from this side and many riders are more skilled in using the whip with the right hand.

It cannot be repeated too often that in the first stage of the *Piaffe* work the rider should be satisfied with a few steps. One should then stop and reward the horse so that it knows what is required of it. Quite gradually the rider will achieve the *Piaffe* exercise for a longer period. If the horse has been taught from the ground to execute the piaffe when advancing, it must be gradually restrained so that it learns to execute the *Piaffe* on the spot. The greatest attention must be paid to the horse performing the *Piaffe* smoothly and regularly, stepping diagonally as at the trot.

No time can be fixed within which the horse can learn the *Piaffe*. It entirely depends on the conformation and the elasticity of the hocks, as to whether it learns the *Piaffe* within a short time, or requires longer to master this exercise. Some horses will show nice, regular steps at the first attempts, but with many horses great patience is required until they learn to engage and bend their hocks.

There is no fixed rule in regard to the execution of the *Piaffe*. The lifting of the fore and hindlegs as well as bringing the hindlegs well under the body depend on the conformation and individuality of the horse. When the horse has been trained from the ground to step regularly, one can start with work under the rider.

The horse that has learnt to step properly without weight will also execute the *Piaffe* under the rider, and will respond to the aids of the legs and whip without undue difficulty.

The horse that has been properly trained from the ground to respond to the whip aids will in many cases perform the *Piaffe* more easily if, at the first attempt, the rider uses his whip. Gradually, with the support of the legs, he teaches the horse to execute the *Piaffe* in response to the legs only. As it is certainly more difficult for the horse to perform the *Piaffe* under the weight of the rider, it is advisable in the first attempts to allow the horse to advance slightly, as this makes it easier for him to bring the hindlegs well forward and it increases the impulsion.

A horse should execute the *Piaffe* in a diagonal way. It must be equally influenced with the legs and reins and be restrained so that it does not deviate with the hindquarters to the left or right. It must be elevated to such a degree that it does not seek a support from the reins. Here the rider's influence on the back of his horse (as described in the chapter, 'Balance') is of the greatest importance. When executing the *Piaffe* the horse should be completely relaxed in its back and should not move with a cramped, tensed back. This has been discussed in detail before. It makes an enormous difference whether the horse executes the *Piaffe* with a supple or with a taut back. Only if the back is supple will it be possible for the horse to step in absolute obedience, to use its hocks in a proper way, to be well on the bit. It must not use the *Piaffe* as a means of resistance, as is so often the case.

The movements of all well trained horses in the *Piaffe* should be regular and smooth, and in no way jerky. Furthermore, in executing the *Piaffe*, the horse should always have so much impulsion and be so well on the bit that the rider is in a position to advance into a trot at any second.

As to the rein and leg aids in the *Piaffe*, one should not try to get every step out of the horse by continuous leg and spur aids; instead it should be influenced by short energetic leg aids and prepared to such an extent that it continues with the *Piaffe* without renewed aid, exactly as in the school trot, when the horse maintains the trot without continuous aids. The hand should be kept in a still, steady position, and must not endeavour to support the *Piaffe* by rein aids. An excessive collection should be avoided. The seat of the rider is of great importance; only when the rider sits absolutely still, is it possible for the horse to execute the *Piaffe* in perfect balance. The rein aids should act on the horse's back by the influence of the rider's back. He should sit quietly and upright and not disturb the movement by weight aids or by swaying in the saddle. As regards carriage and elevation of the horse, the same requirements must be observed as have already been described for the trot (Balance). The elevation should be in accordance with the abilities and behaviour of the horse to the extent that it is induced to relax in its back, and to use the hind-legs in a proper way and bend its hocks.

Understandably, everything does not always work according to plan, as described here. Often one encounters difficulties so numerous and varied that they cannot all be described here. It requires years of practice and routine before the rider is able to school a horse so that it makes the desired progress, and performs the tasks within the time the rider has set himself. It can, however, be said that the more skilled the rider, the less will he fight his horse. He will always present the tasks in such a manner that they can be executed by the horse without brute force. Although I do not propose to mention here the different forms of resistance, I shall now touch upon a few of them.

Piaffe behind the bit. If in the *Piaffe* work insufficient attention has been paid to the horse being properly on the bit with corresponding elevation, and always maintaining the forward impulsion, it will be inclined to overbend, and to be behind the bit. Such horses will hardly respond to the driving aids. Instead, they will use the *Piaffe* as means of resistance and be inclined to rear. In such cases it is primarily necessary to re-establish the forward impulsion. The very moment the horse starts to hesitate by getting behind the bit, it must be influenced by short, strong leg and spur aids, remaining at the same time elevated until it willingly accepts the driving aids, combined with corresponding rein aids, so that it offers no more resistance in its back. As long as the horse executes the *Piaffe* with a stiffened back it will always be inclined to fall back into its old faults and to hesitate. In these cases one should ask for only a very short *Piaffe* and pay strict attention to its maintaining the necessary elevation and forward impulsion. If the horse still hesitates, one has to drive it on immediately until the forward impulsion and the corresponding elevation are regained. Otherwise—I again repeat it—one should be satisfied with a very short period in this exercise and be very careful to practise the horse for a fairly long time in the advancing *Piaffe*, and only when this exercise is firmly established, gradually ask for the *Piaffe* on the spot.

Rearing in the Piaffe. If the horse opposes the aids of the rider by rearing up, an energetic influence immediately becomes necessary which must begin the very moment the horse starts to rear. A skilled rider will find it possible, if the attempt is only a slight one, to drive the horse on by strong whip and spur aids until the horse again accepts the bit. It entirely depends on the rider's experience, whether this fault can be quickly and thoroughly corrected. It is very important that he drives the horse firmly forward with whip and spurs at the very moment the horse stands on its hindlegs; he must not delay until the horse has again touched the ground. By the rider so acting the horse clearly feels that it is impossible to avoid the rider's aids and punishments by rearing. One should be especially careful not to interfere with the reins, as a sensitive horse might fall over backwards by receiving a jerk in the mouth.

Deviating from the Straight Line at the Piaffe. This is caused by keeping the horse too long in the *Piaffe*. As it becomes difficult, if not impossible, for the horse to continue to bend its hocks it tries to evade the rider's aids. In this case the demands in the *Piaffe* should be reduced. The periods of practice should be shortened until the horse becomes quite steady in advancing in the *Piaffe*.

The work of the *Piaffe* is most important for the training of the school horse, for it learns by this exercise better than in any other movement, to bend and engage its haunches. It is induced to supple up its hindlegs, bringing them well forward, which is most useful for all other work of the *Haute École*, and for all the different movements on and above the ground. A horse that has learned to respond in the *Piaffe* to the slightest indications of the rider, and to be supple, light and elevated, will easily find it possible to execute all those short turns, halts and other movements of the *Haute École* that require absolute suppleness and increased bending of the hocks. The proof of a well executed *Piaffe* is that the horse presses neither back nor forward, and that its steps are rhythmical and cadenced. In other words, it is perfectly balanced.

WORK ON THE PILLARS

If the horse has been sufficiently trained from the ground no particular difficulty will be met when it is placed in the pillars. The horse, fitted with a cavesson, and with a leading rein and a special pillar halter, is now led between the pillars and attached to the pillar reins. In this work it is advisable to have an assistant to lead the horse forward by the leading rein or to put it straight, should it step or deviate to one side in the pillars. One should on no account pull with the leading rein, as this would disturb the work and the horse would offer resistance to the continuous tight leading rein. On the contrary, as soon as the horse has regained the desired contact with the pillar reins, the leading rein ought to be quite loose. Just as in the work from the ground, the horse has to be driven forward with the whip from the rear so that it executes a few *Piaffe* steps. At the start these steps will not be very regular, the horse being somewhat hindered by the pillar reins. Great patience and care has to be observed, as clumsy or rough handling in the pillars can easily frighten the horse so that this method is of no use or help to him; it will only cause him to resist. A horse that is standing for the first time in the pillars, with side reins, will usually advance in the *Piaffe* and will find resistance in the pillar reins. This is a very critical moment, and one should not drive the horse roughly forward with the whip. The trainer must wait until the horse has re-gained the necessary calmness, and then he can drive it carefully forward until the desired contact is achieved. This contact has already been discussed previously, and it ought to be the same as in the work from the ground, the pillar reins corresponding to the leading rein or the rider's reins on horseback. A horse that can execute the *Piaffe* obediently will step quietly and willingly on a straight line, without deviating to the right or left with the hindquarters, the pillar reins maintaining a light contact. If a horse should show particular nervousness or unwillingness in the pillars, one should not use force for executing the *Piaffe*, as the strength of the horse is generally greater than the pillar reins or the pillars, and it might lead to unpleasant scenes. In these cases, the horse has not been properly prepared from the ground. One should start again with the ground work and continue with it until the horse has learned to step on the spot in absolute obedience without pillars, and is thoroughly acquainted with whip and rein aids.

In the case of particularly nervous horses it is advisable not to attach the pillar reins at once, but to fit two leading reins (right and left), and then lead the horse into the pillars with the help of two assistants. In this way one can overcome the resistance caused by placing the horse in the pillars and fixing the pillar reins. A horse that has learned to execute the *Piaffe* in this way should, as a pre-caution, first be fitted with one pillar rein, the assistant holding the leading rein on the other side. Alternatively, the trainer should be at the side of the horse, holding the leading rein, and then, when the horse has gained sufficient confidence, attach both pillar reins. The practiçe of placing the horse in the pillars without the preliminary work on the ground is tedious, and calls for a great deal of

PLATE XXV. *Lindenbauer (Vienna) at the Passage on Lipizza Stallion*

PLATE XXVI. *Meixner (Vienna) at the Passage*

PLATE XXVII. *The Author at the Passage in Vienna*

PLATE XXVIII. *The Author at the Passage*

PLATE XXIX. *Levade from the ground where the aids are clearly demonstrated*

PLATE XXX. *The Author at the Levade* PLATE XXXI. *Meixner (Vienna) at the Levade*

PLATE XXXII. *Neumayer (Vienna) executing a splendid, perfect Courb*

PLATE XXXIII. *Capriole*

PLATE XXXIV. *Polak (Vienna) at the Capriole*

skill. The horse must first learn to move its hindquarters to the right and left in response to the whip, so that it is induced to execute a few steps by the sideways movement. It will then gradually produce some steps on the spot and on the straight line. By this method, it will in time learn the *Piaffe* on the spot in response to the whip aids, which are applied in the same manner as in the work from the ground without pillars. As already mentioned, horses which are talented, may also learn the *Piaffe* under the rider without any preliminary work from the ground.

PASSAGE

The Passage (also called Spanish Trot) is the execution of the school trot in its highest perfection. The horse moves in the Passage in perfect collection and elevation, diagonally, with an increased engagement of the hocks and a lowered croup. There is a great difference between the school and the circus Passage which is attained by touching the forelegs with the whip; there is no proper bending of the hocks, the hindlegs are stiff and the steps are irregular. The correct school Passage can be developed from the *Piaffe* or from the school trot, and entirely depends on the ability of the horse. In the Passage an increased elevation and an increased following up of the hindlegs is necessary, and for this reason the horse has to be firmly driven forward from the *Piaffe* or the school trot with high elevation, so that it is induced to execute a few short elevated steps, gaining very little ground. The exact moment when the horse is about to produce one or two cadenced, rhythmical steps must be accurately observed, and it must be induced to carry them out correctly. At this moment the horse should immediately be rewarded and the exercise should be stopped, so that it recognizes clearly that it has fulfilled its task and done well.

The unschooled passage is a movement which horses at liberty execute when excited. A correctly performed passage is one of the most beautiful and pleasing movements of the *Haute École*. The rider must school his horse with special care and exactness, basing his methods on the principles of the classical art of riding.

The more advanced the horse is in its *Piaffe* work, the easier it will learn to execute the Passage in a correct way. If a horse has learned in the *Piaffe* to step forward with a good contact and full of impulsion, it will not be difficult to achieve a few Passage steps by increased driving aids and an increased elevation. The school horse should execute the Passage with great liveliness, and with the maximum impulsion and engagement of the hocks. The rider has to use quite strong driving aids, depending of course on the horse's temperament, in order to achieve a few lively, cadenced steps by the driving and restraining aids. As when schooling the horse in all other movements, it is essential that the first periods of the Passage are short, since these first attempts impose a great strain on the horse. If the periods are too long the horse can quickly become unwilling and obstinate. The main point is that the horse should start the Passage in response to the light aids of the rider and then, from schooling on both reins, later attain the ability to remain in the Passage for longer periods. On no account should the horse stiffen its back or, even worse, swing the hindlegs sideways, which also causes it to swish its tail. When teaching the horse the Passage, the school trot will at first suffer, as the horse has not yet learned the difference between school trot and Passage. It is therefore important to practise the short, rhythmical school trot on a straight line after each period of Passage. In the preliminary stages of the Passage particular attention should be paid to the regularity of the pace. The horse should not be hindered from executing a proper Passage by excessive collection and by aids of the spurs. The rider should not try to support the development of the Passage by rein aids which act backwards; he must achieve the elevation and position in which it is easiest for the horse to execute the Passage in perfect collection and carriage, all resulting from the forward movement.

The faults which occur most frequently in the Passage are as follows:

1. The horse does not accept the bit (is behind the bit). The horse resists by stiffening the back and does not bring the hindlegs properly forward, thus not responding to the leg aids, resulting in irregular steps of the hindlegs.

2. When rushing in the Passage the horse seeks more support from the reins, and therefore cannot maintain the slow cadenced steps; it merely trots on.

In the first case the horse must be corrected in exactly the same way as described in '*Piaffe* behind the bit'. In the second case the horse must be properly elevated, thus being induced to relax in its back, which makes it impossible for it to seek a support from the reins. Should the horse, by rushing forward, revert to a trot, one should not force it into a Passage, but should bring it back to a walk by short, strong, elevating half halts. After the necessary contact and collection has been re-established, the Passage exercise can be resumed. If the horse does not respond to these aids it should be corrected by a short *arrêt* or by reining it back for a few strides.

Finally, I must add that the execution of the Passage depends very much on the conformation of the horse and, consequently, greatly varies. There are horses that execute the Passage with forelegs more bent than other horses, who stretch them out. Both can be regarded as correct. The essential point is that the horse performs the Passage with rhythmical, cadenced steps, full of impulsion and in perfect collection. The croup must be lowered, the hocks well bent and the Passage carried out in a precise, supple, diagonal movement.

PASSAGE ON TWO TRACKS

When the horse is thoroughly confirmed in the Passage (the Spanish Trot) on a straight line, this exercise can be practised on two tracks. It is advisable to start with the shoulder-in, as it is less difficult to maintain the Passage in this movement. One should start with a very slight inside position and only gradually ask for the correct bend. Here too, it is best to continue for short periods only. Should the horse deviate with the quarters, one should take it back to the straight line, and after executing a correct Passage begin again with the shoulder-in. All the other two track movements are developed from the shoulder-in. As for the aids, the horse should move forward with the same light contact as at the school trot, and it should not be irritated by continuous rein and leg aids. These should be applied in such a manner that it learns to carry out longer periods without strong leg aids. These aids, when too often repeated, result in irregular steps of the hindlegs. The other important points of the movements on two tracks have been described in the chapter 'Lateral Work at the Trot'.

LEVADE

The *Levade* is a movement above the ground in which the horse raises the forelegs from the ground and then draws them in, whilst the hindquarters are bent to the maximum and are brought well forward, bearing the entire weight of the body in highest collection and perfect balance.

This school movement is derived from the rearing stallion when at liberty. After years of intensive, systematic training, the horse's muscles are developed to such an extent that it carries its whole weight with its hindlegs. The correctly executed *Levade* is the result of intensive schooling on the principles of the classical art of riding, and greatly differs from the *Circus Levade*, which often consists of rearing up with stiff unbent hindlegs.

The *Levade* is developed out of the *Piaffe*. A horse that has learned to bend its hocks and to bring the hindlegs well forward, is induced by a corresponding restraining influence, to use its hindquarters as sole support, thereby drawing in its forelegs and remaining in this position for some seconds. When learning the *Levade* it is very advantageous, although not absolutely necessary, to start the exercise from the ground, as it is easier for the horse to acquire the proper balance without the weight of the rider. The drawing in of the forelegs should never be attempted by touching them with the whip, but should be the natural result of a perfect collection.

Movements above the ground cannot be demanded from every horse, as they call for a special talent. Such a horse will already show a tendency in the *Piaffe* to rear up with the increased bending of the hindlegs. If it is induced in the work from the ground to bring the hindlegs well under the body and at the same time is restrained by the leading rein, it will attempt to raise its forelegs. This attempt should not be overlooked, and if the horse is sufficiently steady in the *Piaffe* the trainer should make use of it. The horse must be rewarded at once, so that whenever it is required to do so, it reacts to these aids by starting the *Levade*. The polishing up of these first attempts and the achieving of a perfect *Levade* require great knowledge as well as time and patience, since the horse must first be physically developed in the muscles of the hindquarters before it can carry itself in this position.

The most important point of this exercise is that the horse learns to bend its hocks more and more, until it finally executes the *Levade* with completely bent hocks.

This results in the drawing in of the forelegs. If a horse does not draw in its forelegs sufficiently it will then stiffen up in its back in the transition from the *Piaffe* to the *Levade*. This is a sign that it has not been sufficiently schooled in the *Piaffe*. This will show in a hanging down of the forelegs.

Whip and leading rein aids must be well co-ordinated. It will sometimes be necessary to restrain the horse quite firmly with the leading rein, so that it does not adopt the habit of creeping back when raising the forelegs, thus executing the *Levade* with a stiff back and behind the bit. In the first attempts one must take great care that the horse is well on the bit. Once again, it is important not to carry out this exercise for too long a time. In the first lessons the trainer should be satisfied with two or three proper attempts when he should again practise the *Piaffe*. A horse that has once understood the aids to raise the forelegs may regard each increased driving aid as a demand to do so, and may attempt to avoid the influence of the trainer by starting the *Levade* on its own account.

Care must be taken that the horse learns to differentiate exactly between the aids for the *Piaffe* and the *Levade*. As soon as it attempts the *Levade* on its own accord it should be driven forward until it executes the *Piaffe*, the *Piaffe* then being stopped immediately and the horse rewarded so that it clearly understands that it has carried out correctly what is desired of it.

This is an important stage in the work above the ground. A horse should only perform this exercise when he is definitely required to do so by his rider, as a horse which has on several occasions been allowed to execute the *Levade* or *Courbette* of its own accord, will soon be inclined to use it as a means of resistance.

I must again repeat that all movements above the ground should be developed from the *Piaffe*. This sequence of schooling applies equally to horses which are well advanced in their training, because it is in the *Piaffe* that the horse attains a state of the highest collection and perfect suppleness, and this is essential for the correct execution of all movements above the ground.

In the same way as it is practised from the ground with whip and leading rein, the *Levade* is also demanded of the horse in the pillars. Here too, it must execute the *Levade* in response to the increased driving aids, with the difference that the pillar reins replace the leading rein. A horse that has received a good preliminary training from the ground will also execute the *Levade* in the pillars without resistance.

LEVADE UNDER THE RIDER
When the horse has learned to carry out the *Levade* in proper balance with the trainer on the ground, this exercise can then be started under the rider. The aids should be applied in the same way as from the ground. One starts with the *Piaffe*. The horse is then induced by firmer driving and simultaneous restraining aids to increase the bending of the hocks and to carry its whole weight with the hind-

legs. The seat and hands of the rider are again of great importance. The seat should be quiet and steady so that the horse is not disturbed while maintaining the balance with its hindlegs in the *Levade*. The upper part of the body should not be bent forward, but should be almost vertical. Furthermore, the rider's hands should be kept quiet and steady. The contact with the reins should not be changed in the *Levade*, so that the same contact with the horse's mouth is maintained as in the *Piaffe*. If the rider should go forward with his hands, the horse would lose the collection necessary for the *Levade* and it could not maintain its balance. Too strong or restless a contact would irritate the horse's mouth and would induce it to rear up or creep backwards. The upper arm should be kept in slight contact with the body. The rider's back should be braced, so that all rein aids act on the back of the horse, with the result that it is supple and relaxed. The legs should be kept in a quiet position, maintaining a good contact with the horse, so that in the *Levade*, as in the *Piaffe*, heels, hips and shoulder form a straight line. The legs should not move forward or lose contact with the horse, as they act on the hindlegs and maintain the necessary engagement.

As in the work from the ground the horse should execute the *Levade* with a supple back and bent hocks. As it cannot be corrected in the *Levade* itself it must be completely balanced and well in hand before starting the exercise; the proper execution is otherwise impossible. A horse which stiffens its back in the *Piaffe* prior to the *Levade* will never be able to execute a correct *Levade*.

A very frequent fault in the *Levade* is that the horse is not properly on the bit; it stiffens its back and does not draw in the forelegs properly, thus gradually creeping backwards. In this case it should be driven forward in the *Piaffe* before the *Levade* is started, and kept well elevated until it relaxes. Only then should the Levade be required of it. The correct seat of the rider is of the greatest importance.

The most important factor in the *Levade* is the proper following-up of the hindlegs and the increased bend of the hocks. However, as the same results will not be achieved with every horse, the execution will therefore be different; much will also depend on the horse's conformation.

From the *Levade*, the High School jumps are developed. A correct start is therefore most important. Depending upon the ability of the horse, the rider can then concentrate on schooling his horse in special school jumps.

COURBETTE

The *Courbette* is a movement above the ground in which the horse—as in the *Levade*—raises itself from the ground with the forelegs well drawn in, in perfect collection, and then jumps up and lands on its hindlegs without touching the ground with its forefeet. The *Courbette* can actually be described as a jump forward in the *Levade*.

These jumps can be carried out once, twice or several times in succession. In teaching the *Courbette*, the horse is influenced to raise itself from the ground in the same way as described in the *Levade*. The very moment the horse goes up with the forelegs, putting its weight on the hindquarters, it must be both restrained and driven forward so that it leaps up with both hindlegs, jumps forward and lands on his hindlegs in the same position. Just as in schooling for the *Levade* the trainer should start the exercise from the ground. Again it is essential that the horse should be perfectly schooled in the *Piaffe*. When the horse attempts the *Levade* from the *Piaffe*, influenced by the driving aids, it must be induced at this very moment to leap forward on its hindquarters in response to an increased driving aid with the whip above its hocks, the leading rein at the same time acting in a restraining way. It may be necessary to support the jump by increasing the whip aids, so that the horse understands that it has to jump at the very moment it lowers its hindquarters. By holding the horse back with the leading rein the trainer prevents the horse from coming down too early on the forelegs. It is induced to land on its hindlegs in the same position, and only then to touch the ground again with the forefeet. When the horse is thoroughly steady in the *Courbette* from the ground, mounted schooling can be started. This requires, of course, great skill and experience, as the rider has to use his legs quickly and firmly at the moment the horse raises its forelegs, thus causing it to leap forward.

The rein aids must restrain the horse to such an extent that in jumping forward it still lands on its hindlegs. The horse's hocks must be well bent and the back completely relaxed in the *Courbette*, as in the *Levade*, thus achieving a smooth and elastic landing on the hindlegs. One must differentiate carefully between the correct *Courbette* and the *Lançade* in which the horse jumps with stiff hindlegs. In order to achieve a smooth and graceful *Courbette* the rider must act with an absolutely still and steady seat, disturbing his horse neither with his legs nor his hands. He must have full control over his legs and hands and be in a position to use them independently from each other, in order to influence the horse at the right moment. In the *Courbette* the horse should raise its forelegs and jump up mainly in response to the leg aids. It should not be pulled up by the reins. On the contrary, the hands must be kept in a very still position, acting in a passive, slightly restraining way. Everything described in connection with the *Levade*, especially in regard to the rider's seat and influence, also applies to the *Courbette*.

If a horse has learned to execute the *Courbette* once, quietly and correctly, it can be influenced to jump a second time at the moment of landing on the hindlegs by short firm leg aids. After systematic schooling a horse with a good conformation will be able to repeat the leaps several times. It is important to keep the horse on a straight line. Before attempting the *Courbette* the horse has to be well collected and be able to respond to the slightest aids of its rider, as in all other school movements.

CAPRIOLE

The *Capriole* is a movement above the ground in which the horse jumps up with its forelegs well drawn in and kicks out with its hindlegs in a horizontal position in the air and then lands again on the same spot. Horses that respond to whip aids by kicking are most suitable for this movement. It should be practised at first from the ground. A horse which is absolutely firm in the *Piaffe* in the work from the ground, and in the pillars and under the rider, should be influenced to raise its forelegs as described in the *Courbette*. It must learn to go up with the forelegs in response to the driving aids. When it is able in this exercise to raise the front legs in response to the rider's aids and is completely obedient, it must then be taught to kick out.

A horse practising this exercise must be influenced by

firmer aids, with the whip applied to the hindlegs or the croup, so that it responds to these aids by kicking out. After a successful jump it must be rewarded and the work must be stopped. The work itself must be carried out with great calmness and patience and without any force, so that the horse never loses its confidence in its trainer. Only in this way will it execute the *Capriole* obediently. As already mentioned the horse should be almost horizontal at the very moment it kicks out. It is a lesser fault if the hindlegs are lower than the forelegs during kicking out, as in the opposite case, the horse will not raise the forelegs in a proper way and kicks out with a stiff back.

If a horse is inclined to kick out too soon, thus not executing the *Capriole* high enough at the rear, the raising of the forelegs should be practised, not the kicking out. But the raising of the forelegs should not be asked for until the horse has learned to raise the forelegs in response to the rider's restraining aids. The *Capriole* is rightly considered as the most difficult movement above the ground. Like all other High School movements, the *Capriole* should not be practised too often, otherwise the horse resents it and it leads to disobedience.

When the horse has learned to execute the *Capriole* in a correct way, without the weight of the rider, the exercise can be practised while mounted. It is advisable to school the horse at the start in the pillars or from the ground with a light weight in the saddle; achieving this the rider gradually starts the *Capriole* himself. The horse is now influenced by the rider to raise its forelegs—as in the *Courbette* —with both leg and corresponding rein aids; he is then asked to kick out with his hindlegs with the aid of the whip.

Everything described in schooling the *Courbette* applies

also to the *Capriole*, especially where the rider's seat, and leg and rein aids are concerned. The horse should not execute the jump of its own accord, but respond exactly to the rider's aids, otherwise it will eventually perform the *Capriole* incorrectly.

I should also like to mention the 'BALOTADE' which is largely similar to the *Capriole*. For this movement, however, a horse draws in its hindlegs so that the iron of the shoes can be seen.

Finally, I want to emphasize once again that all the school movements above the ground are developed from the *Piaffe*. In this exercise, properly executed, the horse is completely relaxed, perfectly collected and supple. It is now so well balanced that its trainer can school it either for the *Levade* or for other movements of the High School above the ground.

(Centuries ago the *Courbette* and *Capriole* were practised for combat. By means of these jumps the encircled rider could rid himself of his adversaries and the kicking out of the hindlegs prevented them from approaching.)

RICHARD WÄTJEN – HIS LIFE AND CAREER

Richard Wätjen was one of the great masters of the art of riding who have permanently influenced the development of dressage. His successes in dressage tests, his genius as a writer and the lessons to be learnt from his books assure him of a reputation as a first-class horseman who is equally experienced in theory and practice.

The significant and lasting effect of his successful work is explained when one follows his career and stresses the most important events which brought him recognition as a dressage rider.

The individual phases of his life are given briefly. Following his early years in Bremen, he spent a valuable apprenticeship in the Trakehnen and Graditz studs, then he studied as a student-instructor at the Spanish Riding School in Vienna, making a career in riding in Berlin and Munich and after the War, continuing this occupation in Düsseldorf and in the United States.

Wätjen was born on July 9th 1891 in Bremen. His family were merchants and shipowners and horselovers as well. So it is not surprising that he grew up amongst horses and everything to do with them. At ten years old he learnt to ride and was given his own horse.

When he left school he had to make a difficult decision. His parents wanted him to go into his father's shipping business. However this career did not satisfy his enthusiasm for horses and everything to do with them. His parents were both understanding and generous and finally allowed him to study agriculture and hippology. Wätjen became assistant in Trakehnen* where he was able to learn theoretical and practical stud management and agriculture under the direction of the Director, Landstallmeister von Oettingen. A year later he went to the stud at Graditz to learn the management of Thoroughbred horses, under the famous Count Siegfried Lehndorff. Then he received permission to further his career by going to Hoppegarten, Berlin to learn something of the training of racehorses. Hoppegarten was a highly successful training establishment and it was a great advantage to him, that Wätjen was taught by the trainer Day, the care and management of fit horses in training. He learned that top class achievement cannot be obtained without the correct stable management, a lesson that was put to proper use later in his own show stable.

By a lucky chance Wätjen was able to spend his afternoons in Berlin at the Luise Tattersall, where he received riding instruction under the distinguished Oskar Stensbeck, one of the most sought after instructors of his time. Wätjen himself acknowledged his debt to his mentor and to the opinion that riding properly developed was an art in itself. Until then he had never ridden a properly trained horse and for the first time he discovered what it was like to sit on a schooled dressage horse who obeyed his rider's aids with confidence and attention.

He recognised that to reach the standard and skill of a rider like Oskar Stensbeck, one had to possess not only physical talent and performance as a rider but also the same measure of character and intelligence. The last two are, in fact, basic necessities. Throughout his life Wätjen had cause

*For further information, see: "The Flight of the East Prussian Horses" by Daphne Machin Goodall.

to be grateful to Stensbeck and especially to the encouraging advice which was decisive to his future career.

In 1910, he decided to further his studies in Vienna, so that he could become a pupil at the famous Spanish Riding School. Through the kindness and support of both Landstallmeister von Oettingen and Count Siegfried Lehndorff, he was accepted. At that time few pupils and serving officers were accepted, so that it was a great honour to be amongst those who were receiving instruction in the art of classical riding.

Wätjen met Maj. Julius Walzer, one of the last serving German officers to be posted to the Spanish Riding School, who was, a year later, to take over the direction of the school stables in Hannover. The outbreak of World War I ended this command after only a few months.

The atmosphere of a steady, high standard of work and the active transmission of a strictly observed method made a tremendous impression on Wätjen. His conviction was strengthened by observation and experience: A great rider requires not only exceptional skill, great sympathy and the ability to react but also a very firm mental attitude which is based upon reliability of character. Wätjen rode under the instruction of the Chief Riding Master Johann Meixner, who had been at the Spanish Riding School from 1885–1916 and who was then director.

Meixner knew how to combine kindness with strict control. In Wätjen's opinion he was a God-given horseman. He rode in complete harmony and with great elegance. His horses went with a light contact and great activity and executed their movements in the most exact manner. The example set by this exceptional instructor describes the quality of work which was later characteristic of Wätjen's method of training his own horses and for his unmistakable manner of presenting them in dressage tests.

The change to pure School riding was at first difficult. But the new pupil soon learnt to appreciate the spirit of the Spanish Riding School and the customs which are bound up in tradition. He took his education in Vienna very seriously and described his progress: "Often when my friends were away at the weekend, visiting the Summering, I stayed behind alone because I would have been too tired on Monday at 7 a.m. Thus the winter passed. I progressed and gained the confidence of my instructors, was given better stallions. When my mother visited the School with the German Ambassador, the Chief Instructor allowed me to ride his famous stallion Favori Ancona. When I had completed the exercises and had produced a levade, my mother begged Herr Meixner to mount the stallion, whereupon with the gesture of a cavalier, he explained, he could not have done better."

In 1912, Wätjen had his first show success on a horse he had trained. He was the only civilian and rode a half-bred Hungarian mare, gaining fourth out of 47 competitors. In August 1914, the pleasant and carefree time in Vienna came to an end. War had broken out. Wätjen was excused army service for the next two years and worked instead at a job connected with the army. Most of the instructors had been called up. When Wätjen reported to the office of the Director in 1916, to help out at the Spanish Riding School, he was invited by the then Director, Prince Pálffy to become a guest instructor. He was very pleased at this distinction. Young stallions were allotted to him and he produced them at public performances.

Meixner's successor was Maritz Herold and he and Count Rudolf von der Straten were responsible that the Riding School did not have to close down in 1918. Besides working with the Chief Instructor Meixner, Wätjen had also worked with other great artists. Senior Instructor Gottlieb Polak, who was a great horseman, had been at the Spanish Riding School since 1917. In 1921 the Riding School was taken over by the State and with a heavy heart, Wätjen had to leave his beloved Vienna where he had spent twelve years studying the art of riding of which he was now a master. At first, owing to the depression, he worked in a bank in Bremen, but horses and riding had become so much a part of his life that he decided to go back to Berlin there to build up a Riding School in the Tattersall Beerman.

This decision was to prove of tremendous value for the future of dressage in Germany. This discipline had begun to take on a clearer form and with the work of instruction of famous riders such as Oskar Stensbeck, Felix Bürkner, August Staeck, Otto Lörke and Richard Wätjen, some of whom are known to English dressage enthusiasts, it soon reached a high *niveau*.

All these exceptionally good instructors worked in Berlin, the city that was to lead Germany's equestrian enthusiasts. In 1932 Felix Bürkner founded a Riding School in Düppel and he managed to encourage Wätjen to take part in dressage instruction, in which academic courses were regularly held.

In preparation for the 1936 Olympic Games he went to Tattersall Tiergarten and then to Munich-Riem, where the Olympic Games were held in 1972.

He was responsible for the instruction and education of a great number of first-class and successful horses and riders and he, himself, was numbered amongst Germany's top dressage riders. With the mare Haustochter and Donner II he won 13 dressage contests and as well in 1928 he had won the Olympic Dressage Contest in Aachen, also with Haustochter.

During the following years Wätjen was numbered amongst the four most successful dressage riders in Germany and in 1935 he again won an Olympic Dressage competition. Equal with the Swede Lt. von Adlerkreutz on Teresina, and riding Burgsdorff he was placed above Otto Lörke on the later Olympic winner Kronos.

He then moved to the Cavalry School in Hannover and was responsible for preparing Captain Viebig and Burgs-dorff. Later General Viebig wrote of his instructor: "His style of riding and his instruction were a mirror of his character and his attitude to life, clear, straightforward and ambitious. An attentive and interested pupil could learn a lot from Richard Wätjen as a person and as a horseman."

With his international reputation, he took over the position as instructor to the U.S. Three Day Event Team after the War and he was in charge of 40 horses and 10 officers who had their headquarters in Munich-Reim. He was immensely successful. The U.S. Three Day Event Team won the 1948 Olympic Gold Medal.

Then in 1952 he came to England for eight months to instruct the British Team and Col. V. D. S. Williams wrote the foreword to the first English edition of this book.

After a few years further instruction in Düsseldorf, Wätjen went to the United States, first as a private in-structor and then to the U.S. Equestrian Team in Gladstone, New Jersey, where he was enormously successful. The secretary of the U.S. Combined Training Association had the following to say: "It is an exceptional physical as well as mental achievement for a man of seventy to be able to get a horse through the difficult requirements of an advanced test, when, in order to do so, he has to be able to stand and instruct in the school for many hours a day. The United States can consider themselves lucky to have such a man in this country."

This description of Richard Wätjen's life and work produces the picture of a master who was amongst those horsemen who gave Germany a place in the world after 1918 and who helped to improve international dressage. He was appreciated in two spheres: his success as a competitor in dressage tests, as a trainer of first-class dressage horses and as an instructor who knew how to put over convincing instruction. At the same time he was a very knowledgeable writer and he can be counted amongst those people who have earned our thanks for his theory of equestrianism contained in the books on dressage which appeared between the wars. The remarkable thing about Wätjen is the fact that he belonged to both groups mentioned above: the combination of complete skill in the saddle and the mental achievement of grasping the lessons of dressage and in producing this in a consistent system.

His style of riding made Wätjen a typical representative of the Viennese school whose fundamentals were and are contained in the "Directives for the execution of the methodical procedure for training horse and rider", as laid down by Field-Marshall Holbein von Holbeinsberg and Director J. Meixner in 1898. At the same time he combined with the "Directives" the German interpretation of dressage riding which was developed by Steinbrecht in 1884 in the publication "Gymnastics for the Horse".

When one observed Wätjen at exercise or at shows, his immaculate seat was at once evident—confirmed also in many photographs—and the influence of this seat on his horses ridden accurately and energetically straight forward. He understood to perfection how to make his horses respond decisively but he never indulged in clumsy aids which have nothing in common with classical riding. His sensitivity in giving the necessary aids to improve balance, pace and oscillation at the correct and exactly right moment, without interfering with the purity of movement and straightness, was especially marked. His ability to hold his horses together with his back and legs enabled him to keep the horses's hindlegs 'under him' and thereby to produce cadence and movement to the highest degree.

Apart from Wätjen's extraordinary conscientious and artistic work, probably the secret of his success lay in the fact that he never asked his horses to perform an exercise for which they were not ready. Because of this he had considerable advantages over those who trained and educated their horses too quickly in order to achieve doubtful ends. The usual consequences—damage to the horse's soundness and deficiencies in the basic movements or in the horse's ability to carry a rider (balance)—speak decisively for Wätjen's way of training and against every divergent method. Having learnt from Meixner's example he knew exactly how to make the most of work on the ground. One was able to observe both in the Spanish Riding School and with his own horses, that they were completely relaxed and from this the mastery with which they developed the piaffe—the trot on the spot.

Seunig said of his instruction: "Absolutely objective even matter-of-fact, Wätjen was against the platitudes of officialdom, although they did not prevent him from allowing his talents to shine."

His own words to his pupils are perhaps characteristic of Wätjen's mental-ethical interpretation of the art of riding and attitude to horses:—

"Never deceive yourselves when working. It is not he who is always finding excuses for his own faults but he who unmistakably accepts real work and with a genuine love of horses sticks to it, so that after long and devoted work he gets near to his desired goal. Every genuine rider knows that learning is not the end and it is just this recognition which binds him for his entire life to the art of riding. You should love your horses without spoiling them. Take the trouble to find your way into your horse's mind without trying to make it human. Only those can become experts who are in tune and as one with their horses both physically and mentally."

The way in which Wätjen set himself and his work to reach the highest standards is an example to everyone who hopes to follow this profession.

Wätjen died on 13.1.66 after a short illness, at Bergisch-Gladbach, where he had been staying over Christmas in his daughter's house. He had been thinking of returning to Germany to continue his work for the encouragement of classical dressage. With the death of Richard Wätjen there died one of the greatest horsemen, as successful in the saddle as he was as an instructor and author.

He was the last of those who had formulated the rules of dressage during the 20's and 30's. Wätjen belonged to the group of five who were internationally recognised in German dressage. Oskar Stensbeck, August Staeck, Felix

Bürkner, Otto Lörke and himself. Few other people achieved such accomplished results and successes after the War. They were Frau K. Franke, F. Gerhard and F. Stecken.

Col. R. Abé wrote of him: "Richard Wätjen is no more. Amongst us his spirit will remain alive—the spirit of chivalry, and also the shining image of one of the representatives of classical dressage of the highest order. A horseman and a master whose great art was only exceeded by his immensely valued human characteristics. Amongst these we counted the superiority of his convictions, his personal modesty and straightforwardness, his reliability and his loyalty. Horsemen and women all over the world mourn his passing, and his memory will be honoured as long as a horseman puts his foot into the stirrup."

ALBERT STECKEN.